ROBERT THEODORIDIS

VELOCITY

UNLEASHING YOUR POTENTIAL & TRANSFORMING DREAMS INTO REALITY

@ROB_THEO_

www.robtheo.com

Copyright © 2024 Robert Theodoridis
ISBN: 978-1-923078-37-6

Published by Vivid Publishing
A division of Fontaine Publishing Group
P.O. Box 948, Fremantle
Western Australia 6959
www.vividpublishing.com.au

A catalogue record for this
book is available from the
National Library of Australia

CONTENTS

PREFACE

This book is designed to unlock the shackles of unwanted beliefs and limitations. It's about assisting you in reaching heights you've never imagined and embracing the boundless possibilities that lie in every moment. The advice in this book is a culmination of my life's experiences, including my time in prison, my biggest mistakes in business and the lessons I learned along the way. All aimed at fortifying your mind to be relentless.

Believe in the power of your dreams; the mind can achieve what it dares to conceive. Imagine a future where every limitation you've faced becomes a stepping stone to unprecedented success, where the barriers to your dreams crumble before your determined efforts. This isn't about small steps or minor tweaks; it's about a seismic shift in how you approach your life, goals, purpose, and the very fabric of your potential. Carry and read this book often to remind yourself what it takes to experience a quantum leap.

The journey you're about to embark on doesn't require the Herculean effort you might expect. Instead, it offers a smarter, more intuitive path to excellence that's been hidden in plain sight. You may be operating at a fraction of your capacity, not yet unveiling the full magnitude of your capabilities. Whether it's personal satisfaction, professional achievement, or a blend of both, you've only begun to explore the vast landscapes of success.

But what if the barriers you've faced were merely illusions? What if the keys to a life of extraordinary achievement and fulfilment are already in your hands, waiting for the courage to turn them? If you knew you could not fail, how far would you go? This book isn't just a guide; it's a gateway to a new realm of possibilities. A realm where your dreams are not just possible but inevitable, if you learn to break free of any deep-seated limiting beliefs.

Prepare to be captivated by a narrative that doesn't just aim to inspire but to ignite a transformation that resonates on a global scale. This isn't just about personal development, growth, mindset, and business; it's about redefining what's possible for you. It's time to peel back the layers that have been holding you back - for good. Be prepared. The layers might be so deep that you never knew they existed. It might trigger truths that you have never wanted to face - until now. It might take you to a dark place. Just remember, without darkness there is no light: And without light, there is no darkness. The universe is divinity in motion and is governed by polar opposites. The quicker we embrace this, the quicker your quantum leap will unveil in your life. My advice? Make those darkest moments your allies through self-acknowledgement, acceptance, accountability, and being true to oneself.

You'll notice I have placed 'Forge an unstoppable mindset' as chapter 1. I believe we need to train ourselves from the neck up first before we endeavour to achieve something big. Once you can grasp and understand the power of the mind – the rest will flow congruently.

As the next chapter awaits, Velocity is designed to create the speed necessary to make monumental movements in your life. The question isn't whether you're ready for this journey; it's whether you're prepared to meet the person you were always meant to be on the other side.

Are you ready for this?

Buckle up. Let's go.

1

FORGE AN UNSTOPPABLE MINDSET

Get ruthless about your mindset. It's the engine room for sanity, liberation, prosperity and growth. This chapter is close to my heart as it was the catalyst in developing a transformative shift within my beliefs. It made me realize what we are truly capable of. I'm dedicated to unravelling the essence of such an unstoppable mindset, a trait that transforms obstacles into stepping stones and every adversity into opportunity. It's about cultivating a spirit so resilient and a will so unyielding that every challenge faced is another chance to prove your mindset is fortified for anything that comes your way. I truly mean this, as I have lived it. Over and over.

At the heart of this transformative journey is the understanding that resilience is not a gift bestowed upon a fortunate few but a forged characteristic, shaped in the fires of personal trials and tribulations. If you feel that you're not quite there yet in your journey or endeavours, it's okay. It's about developing a core of steel, not through avoiding challenges, but by embracing them as necessary elements of your growth. Every challenge in your life is an opportunity to strengthen and increase your mindset and resiliency. Your own mental threshold. You essentially raise the bar with every victory. It sets a precedent for any future trials. It increases your thermostat that little bit extra. And I urge you to embrace the trials when they arrive. Trust me, they will come eventually.

Life will undoubtedly throw us hurdles, bumps, and heartbreak. It's important to start priming your mind that you will encounter seasons of loss and defeat. It's also imperative to remember that life will also bless you with many seasons of triumph and success. The quicker we prime our minds that this will undoubtedly happen, the better we are for it. And I don't mean this lightly. It will literally change the trajectory in your life and how you handle every decision (whether big or small) in your journey moving forward.

The mind is a magical organ that has the ability to create or detonate. I remember the moment I lost full control of my mind. It's such a painful and debilitating experience that I don't wish it upon anyone. I honestly thought there was no turning back. I felt as though I'd reached a depth so low that I could never climb out. Every day felt like a struggle, every moment a battle against my own mind. It was a darkness so profound that it seemed endless, swallowing every shred of hope and joy. But in that abyss, I discovered a strength I never knew I had. It was in the deepest despair that I found the spark of resilience, the flicker of a fighting spirit. In order to transform my situation, I understood the only way out was to firstly embrace the pain. This journey taught me that our lowest points are not our end but the beginning of our rise. It's in these moments that we redefine our limits, rewrite our stories, and rise to greatness. Remember, no matter how deep the fall, the climb back up is always within reach. You are stronger than you think, and your story is far from over.

Sitting in a cockroach-infested cell at Long Bay Maximum Security Prison in Sydney, I found myself numb, lost, and deep in thought. It wasn't just any thoughts. I had become so petrified of prison and my surroundings that I started creating these recurring imaginary scenes in my mind that weren't true. I found out later that this is a mental condition called 'Intrusive Thoughts.' Yet even though there was a one in a billion chance that these fabricated events would never happen in real life, my own mind started to believe it. It had repeatedly been playing in my head. Like a broken record stuck and skipping on the same tune, over and over.

My fight-or-flight sympathetic nervous system was on overdrive continuously for months on end. It started to break me down to the point where I had given up. I wanted to end my life. In these moments of despair, the pain was unbearable. It was debilitating and ruthless. Intrusive thoughts are real. Very real. And if you don't know how to control them, they'll start controlling you. Mental health can lead an individual to places they haven't been before. In a short space of time. Although negative thoughts can be detrimental to your health, there are effective methods you can use to combat them and take full control. For good.

Intrusive thoughts were only one part of the equation. The reason why these thoughts literally 'stuck' and manifested in my head so intensely was because they were mixed with deep feelings of emotion. This created a mental and psychological imprint. It stuck like the strongest glue you could ever imagine. I clearly remember the cold rush of blood going through my body when they officially rooted themselves deep within my brain. I remember the moment so vividly. I was literally paralysed for a few minutes. The minutes turned into hours, weeks, months, and continued for almost two years. The eerie feeling of being incarcerated for life in prison numbed my soul. The words 'never to be released' haunted my mind. Could you imagine? I thought to myself. It literally traumatized and plagued me. I was already suffering from PTSD (post-traumatic stress disorder) and now this was compounding the situation and testing my mental capacity which was already shot. Remember, I was raised in a good Greek family and I had never been in trouble with the law. Ever. Now I found myself in one of the oldest, seediest, and unhygienic prisons in the country. From one extreme to another, literally overnight. If I had to paint a picture of what hell looked like, this was it.

You're probably wondering what these thoughts were?

Well, because I never wanted to see the inside walls of prison ever again, my mind started thinking of all of the unrealistic ways I could find myself back inside after my release. At this stage, I had no idea how long I was looking at. It was at the start of my journey, and I was stuck in remand. The remand yard is where individuals are kept that are going through the court system and awaiting sentencing. The devil knew I was vulnerable, so the little pheasant thought it was a great time to attack. Whilst I felt hopeless with my back against the wall. I was up for the fight – one day at a time.

The worst of these thoughts was me thinking and imagining I would commit a heinous crime whilst 'sleepwalking' when I was free and back home. Even though I hadn't experienced sleepwalking since my youth, it's amazing how the mind can come up with the weirdest things in an attempt to defend the unrealistic risk and consequence. The chances of me sleepwalking and grabbing a knife or something of that nature to hurt someone was absurd. I started to believe it though. So, I thought of ways to eliminate the situation. Lock myself in a room at night? Get someone to cuff me to the bed? Sleep alone in my own place? The list went on.

What if this was truly possible? What if I unknowingly hurt someone I love? What if the Police didn't believe me that it was an accident?

The term 'head miles' in prison refers to someone over-thinking and causing themselves unnecessary pain through their thoughts. My brain odometer would have easily clocked a million miles with all the fucked-up thinking that was going on in my head.

The repeating 'what if's' that rolled in my mind were hurting me. Badly. The more you try to eliminate these unwanted and abnormal thoughts, the more they dig deeper and take hold, like the root system of a wild fig tree which are spread long and deep. When you're in this state, it seems like all hope is lost. But that's not the case. It can be reversed much easier than you think. I didn't know this at the time, but it was trial and error for me. Looking back, I know I was being guided in the right direction in search of the right answers.

I remember spending my last three months before my release in a minimum-security prison in Muswellbrook,

NSW. They do this to normalize and prepare inmates before being released back into society. At this stage, I was still broken and not well, however, I was keeping myself busy by working as much as I could and training as hard as I could. This enabled me to sleep well and keep the daily dose of endorphins filtering through my body. It was my natural drug. I hadn't revealed my pain or anguish to any inmates during my time in prison. I never wanted to burden anyone with my issues, even though I was always there for others. I knew everyone had their own battles to face. I even had the hardest and most violent inmates cry on my shoulder at times. It gave me strength being able to help others.

One afternoon, I started a conversation with a fellow inmate whom I used to work with during our work release program. He told me how he suffered from Tourette's and intrusive thoughts. My eyes and ears lit up like a lion ready to pounce on its prey. Every detail he was explaining was the exact symptoms I had been facing for so long. I felt a sense of normality for a moment. I didn't feel alone anymore, thinking I was the only one going through this pain. The confusion and fabricated tales that tormented me for so long started to show cracks and signs of weakness. I began to understand this condition was common amongst many people.

Later that afternoon, I had a hunch to go visit the prison library to see if I could find any books that had any information on psychology and mental health. I wasn't expecting much as the resources were very limited. To my amazement, I found a book that detailed this exact condition. Coincidence? Definitely not. 'When the student is ready, the teacher will appear.' This was one of those instances where I was nudged and guided on the right path, at the right time. As I read these pages, tears rolled down my face. That day, whilst reading this book – I had one of the biggest breakthroughs.

It made me think: How many people are going through this pain in their lives? I promised myself from that moment, once I got through prison and completely healed, I would serve humanity in any way possible to help and assist those who feel like all hope is lost. I wanted to be the one to elevate others. It's also one of the main reasons why I'm writing this book. If you feel like you're going through a rough time or struggling mentally, you're not alone and you're not going crazy. It takes a special individual to express their vulnerabilities and admit they have a problem or need help. Never allow pride to get in the way of the healing process. Acceptance is pure liberation and fulfillment. Don't be ashamed or embarrassed to speak about anything. There is not one person on this planet who doesn't go through some type of hardship or trauma. It's what you do during and after those moments that makes a profound impact in your life. If you can control your thoughts and emotions, you will control the outcome. And that becomes exceptionally powerful.

If you have gone through trauma or feel as though you have lost control of your mind and the thoughts that come with it, these are the main areas to focus on first. They were the exact fundamentals that uplifted and brought me out of despair.

1. **Never suppress or ignore any unwanted thoughts.** I know this may sound counterintuitive, illogical, hypocritical, and weird but hear me out for a moment. Have you ever heard the term, 'speech is silver, silence is gold?' For those that haven't, this purely means that 'less is more'. It shows you're in control. You should never act and respond erratically when your emotions are high. Your mind should always be stronger than your feelings, otherwise, we can make premature and irrational decisions based on temporary emotions. So, when an unwanted thought enters your mind, the first step is to let it in. Remain calm and acknowledge the thought or thoughts you are experiencing. Accept it for what it is. Remember, it's just a thought. You can voice this out loud or even say it under your breath if you find yourself in a crowded place. Say, "I acknowledge these thoughts at this moment. However, the likelihood of this occurring ('the event'), is extremely unlikely to happen. These thoughts don't serve me and I will focus my energy on the thoughts that do serve me and align with my values, beliefs, and true purpose."

By doing this, not only have you established authority by being calm and not responding erratically to your negative emotions. But you have also displayed your dominance by making the conscious choice of giving them access in the first place. Reaffirming it with your own voice out loud is a profound and effective way to affirm your superiority. This creates an imprint in your mind and body. It shows you're in control. If you do this enough times, your mind will be consciously aware to pick up the cues and know how to process each scenario. It won't allow it to be the dominating factor anymore. Think of it as the most powerful antivirus software embedded in your mind. It creates a filter and gives you the conscious choice to continue or let it go. Writing your thoughts down on paper or even journaling is a strong way to realize that your negative thinking is likely utter nonsense and 99.9% fiction. If it looks ridiculous on paper, try reading it back to yourself. It'll no doubt sound hideous. With the statistics on mental health rising more than ever, it's up to us to change our own paradigm and how we should think for the betterment of our own health. Medication and suppressing the true root cause of the issue, will only give a temporary solution. We don't want temporary solutions with more of the same. We need solid, long-lasting, and tangible solutions that will mitigate the risk of you spiralling out of control.

2. **If you ever find yourself in a bad way, mentally, the quickest way to change your physiology is to move your body.** Exercise might seem like a simple solution, however, most of us opt to take the cheap and easy dopamine hit through other means. Again, this will only give you temporary relief. It's a band-aid solution. Your body gets you to the battlefield, but it's the mind that wins the fight. There were hundreds of times I wanted to stay in bed during my darkest hours of mental anguish. Especially when it was freezing cold. In prison, there were many times we would be locked in our cells for days. One time in Goulburn we were locked in for five days straight. If you were claustrophobic, you'd be screwed. Even though I was stuck in confinement, I still showed up. Alone. In my cell. Training harder than ever. I never wanted to give in and take the easy route. That's not me. And I want to believe that's not you either. Don't treat life as a rehearsal. If you have the ability to make a change, don't procrastinate. Stop thinking that your time here in the physical realm is unlimited. Once this experience is over, we're not getting another shot. Make it count and don't be a passenger. Be the CEO in your own life and take charge. We all have the ability to alter our state and emotions through physical motion. It's a simple yet effective way to get out of those shitty periods, quickly. The beautiful part about it, it costs nothing. It's free medicine. It also gives

you the ability to strengthen your mind, body, confidence, and build the fortitude you deserve. If someone can train hard in a tiny prison cell and resist the spiritual, mental, physical, and emotional warfare, there should be no excuse when you're healthy and have the liberty to do what you please. We all have a choice. What will yours be?

3. **All our lives, we've been conditioned to believe that fear is something to be afraid of.** There's been a huge misconception on this topic, and this is about to change. Start making fear your friend. Your ally. Your secret weapon. Don't take a backward step every time you need to face something that's been holding you back. An element of fear in your life is actually very healthy. It nudges you into the realm of uncharted possibilities. It takes you to places you've never been before, and it gives you the adrenaline to act. By taking action, it gives you a much greater chance to crystallize your visions into reality. Next time the butterflies are turning in your stomach and you're starting to feel uncomfortable, understand that fear is giving you cues. It nudges you towards the edge. Use this energy for the power of pursuit. I have come up with a new acronym for fear. I hope this will change your mindset on this powerful four-letter word. We can either: 'Fear Everything And Run', or 'Face Everything And Rise'. If you have a choice

to run or rise, choose the latter. The payoff is far greater.

It's also important to mention, our minds are a crucial weapon in overcoming adversity. Your mind will also remember the last three times how you reacted in difficult situations. If you've run away every time adversity hits - your mind will have the instinct to run and not face it because that's what it has been conditioned to do. Don't be the one that runs all the time. Face it. Overcome it. Build that mental muscle and elevate your resiliency threshold to new heights. This will take daily discipline and commitment. It takes a special individual to break generational cycles. That person could be you. We are infinite beings that have untapped potential. Discover the undiscoverable and it will change your life forever.

Many of my victories have come from an unwavering faith in God, having the tenacity to see things through, family, and physical exercise. The right mixture of these things literally got me through the toughest moments. Whether you're in prison or not, life has so many different forms of adversities. These can come in the form of losing a loved one, a marriage breakdown, trauma, illness, or bankruptcy to name a few. Life-changing events can shake someone to the core and expose their vulnerabilities. It also can expose and ignite something special inside of you. It's the inner strength that was dormant for so long but now comes to life. The fire starts burning and you realize there's a long reservoir of fuel that is ready to be used. If you channel that energy in the correct manner, your mindset will never be the same. You'll become a fearless warrior that can withstand the biggest battles. I urge you to gain a strong understanding of this chapter as it can be the catalyst to materialize a fortified mindset for the rest of your life.

2

SUSPEND LIMITATIONS & CHANGE YOUR LANGUAGE

This chapter is undoubtedly the most important of this book. Without a clear and deep understanding, it can make you feel like a ship in deep waters with no clear destination in sight, continuing to go around in circles, thinking something will change by mere accident.

Every single person has been raised with certain beliefs, traits, and assumptions. These paradigms are deeply ingrained in our subconscious mind, affecting our day-to-day decision-making. We have been programmed by our parents, siblings, teachers, and peers. We have come to the conclusion that conventional thinking is the truth and nothing else exists. Unfortunately, most of the bullshit paradigms that have been ingrained in us are lies. Sad to say, but true. If there's one important lesson I want you to take away from this book, it's this: question everything you see and hear, and don't follow the status quo.

I love my parents deeply, and they gave me everything I could ever ask for. But, like most loving parents they raised me and my siblings as best they knew how. It wasn't their fault they weren't perfect and knew everything there was to know about parenthood. They migrated from Greece to Australia in the 1960s and came from very little, not knowing a word of English upon arrival. They certainly didn't know about limiting beliefs and shifting paradigms. However, as each generation passes by, it becomes our duty to improve and elevate our children so they are more aware, equipped and conscious of everything that surrounds them.

Becoming aware of your limiting beliefs will kickstart a complete transformation in your life. When you make the leap, you will find out so many new things about yourself. The process will be mind-blowing and may hurt at first. Just remember that a caterpillar goes through temporary pain when the process of metamorphosis occurs. Afterwards, it becomes this aesthetic beauty, just as mother nature intended it to be—free and beautiful.

As a kid, I thought wealth was only for a select few and seemed rare in my eyes. I was always told I would never be good enough in so many areas, and because of this,

I was extremely introverted and lacked confidence as I grew older. This became a problem because I started to look for external sources such as alcohol and recreational drugs to numb and suppress the pain during my twenties. I thank God every day for blessing me with an amazing body which held up during those interesting seasons. I know many individuals who have done far less but didn't survive.

I take full accountability of all the actions in my life. But just like the caterpillar, we turn into completely different beings as we progress through the years. Unrecognisable, we elevate to the 2.0 version, 3.0 version, and beyond. Our internal program and beliefs should be getting a major upgrade every single year. We should never be too naive, thinking we know everything there is to know about life, personal development, and business. My late father used to always say that the best teacher you could ever find is life itself. How right he was.

To change your paradigms and core beliefs, you first have to understand the importance of identifying the root cause of the issue. Where have your beliefs come from? How did they form? Without it, any work you do on yourself won't be apparent and will hinder its poten-tial. So, what do I mean by paradigm and core beliefs? It's the negative self-talk that you have used all your life, combined with the false accusations you believe to be true about yourself, that can cause numerous negative results in your everyday life. Most times, you may not even know you have them.

Imagine if we were all designed without limitations on our ability to think and achieve. Whether you believe in a higher power or not, it's hard to think that our existence is meant for constant pain, torment, and suffering. Life is a journey of diverse emotions and seasons. It's these very ups and downs that make our experiences rich and fulfilling, preventing life from becoming plain, boring, and monotonous.

I'm not saying all of us have the potential and genes to run a 100m in under 10 seconds. There are physical limitations among us. However, our minds have the ability to create substantial quantum leaps. Imagination is everything. It's the preview of life's coming attractions. If you can see it in your mind, you can create it in the physical form. Visualize, then capitalize.

The distance between the imagined vision and the physical realm you create is the distance between your ears. When you think about it, that's not very far. A mere 15 cm approximately, depending on how big your head is from ear to ear. The human brain is a supernatural organ that defies logic. Information in the brain can travel up to an impressive 428 kilometres per hour. When a neuron is stimulated, it generates an electrical impulse that travels from cell to cell at lightning speeds. Electricity is always in and all around us - continuously. When an enlightened idea is sparked by the limbic system in the brain, it's a cue for you to capture that moment. Once an idea is born, it's the gateway to endless possibilities. In order to start the process of constructing the tangible form, you need to know where you are, where you are going, then take action. Mere wishful thinking is not enough.

We have phenomenal mental faculties; therefore, we need to shift our energies to create new paradigms that serve us. If the old paradigms remain in control, we're toast. You can try harder, you can read all the self-help books, but if you don't cut the cord completely, especially from those you surround yourself with daily who are negative, you will constantly feel stuck. And the vicious cycle continues.

As mentioned earlier, we are powerful human beings made up of divine energy vibrating at a very high frequency. We are so much more than just matter which occupies time and space. Why is it that we place all these constrictive limitations on ourselves when the only limitations that are bestowed upon us are the ones we have perceived to be true? And most of the time, this has been pushed on us by others from a young age, which has stuck ever since.

It's time to break the shackles and eliminate the ignorance that might be hindering you. Have you ever caught yourself saying one of these phrases to yourself or to someone else throughout your life, or been on the receiving end by someone else?

- You're not good enough

- Money doesn't grow on trees

- Money is the root of all evil

- No news is good news

- Stick to what you know

- You're a dreamer

- I told you so

- You'll never amount to anything

- I can't afford it

- It's not possible

- Who do you think you are?

- I'm not worthy

- Slow and steady wins the race

Start using words and phrases that serve you, benefit you, and align with who you truly are. Being pessimistic, narcissistic, and negative is detrimental to your health and growth—emotionally, physically, spiritually, and financially. You deserve more.

Anxiety, depression, and self-doubt are the biggest thieves that have ever existed. Suspend disbelief and if you want to doubt something, doubt your current beliefs and limitations. Get rid of the mental junk and scepticism that has been based on conventional and rational thinking.

I want you to start being extremely cautious and conscious of the language you project into the world, as well as the language you use on yourself. You may think that it's not so harmful, and what you say is only expressed in a tongue-in-cheek way, but in actuality, you're probably creating a belief without you even knowing it. Your subconscious mind will deem it to be true the more times you express and voice it. The mind doesn't know the difference between 'perceived reality' and 'definite reality.'

Remember my encounter with intrusive thoughts? They were fictional thoughts and scenarios, yet my mind believed them over a period of time. Let me remind you this was done in a very short duration. It didn't take long before my mind started to believe them. Can you imagine going years on end and not being aware of the damage being caused within your own headspace? It was the repetition mixed with emotion that amplified the experience. These imaginary thoughts even had the ability to affect my physiology. This shows the magnitude of the brain's power and how it can materialize, whether positive or negative.

To understand how we can start to tackle and change our own language and paradigms: we must really pay attention to these three factors below.

1. **Start by making the subconscious more conscious.** This allows you to be more alert and aware of your surroundings and who you interact with. This is a great starting point. Pay close attention to the language people use when they speak to you directly, and also take note of how you're responding to someone. You'll start to find that you'll consciously 'catch' unwanted words that are negative and no longer serve you. You can politely correct those you interact with (to make them aware), or you can just choose to remain silent. I would personally share the love and wisdom to better my fellow brother or sister.

   Start using phrases such as "I can," "I am," and "I will" instead of "I can't," "I'm not," or "I won't." Your vocabulary should be filled with words like love, gratitude, optimism, success, inspiration, confidence, humility, and elevation. Get out of that negative and pessimistic frame of mind. Words have the energy and power to help, heal, hurt, humiliate, and humble. Our words have the power to build people up and give them life. They also have the ability to tear people down and bring them death. Choose wisely. It may take some time to train yourself to 'catch' these moments. However, once it clicks, it sticks. Stay aware and nurture your inner flare.

2. **When you have made the conscious decision to elevate yourself in your personal and professional life, your environment must change.** This includes the people you surround yourself with and what you consume on a daily basis. One of the worst things you can do as a high achiever and entrepreneur is to consume everything on the news, read every newspaper, and spend all day binge-scrolling on social media. High achievers don't have time to worry about stuff that's out of their control and certainly shouldn't be worried about what everybody ate for breakfast. Be a creator, not just a consumer.

    You need to start surrounding yourself with individuals who share similar values, morals, and ethics. Your circle of allies should be people you look up to and can ask for advice when it's needed. You want people who elevate you and vice versa, not people who are leeches and suck the life out of you. Turn off notifications to eliminate or minimize distractions, and when you consume any form of content, make it count. Use it for personal growth—a way to educate and amplify your bandwidth. If you surround yourself with negativity, you will start to absorb it, and I certainly don't want that for you.

Never feel bad if you have to walk away from certain relationships. And if you can't cut the cord completely, limit your interactions with these individuals. Never let anyone make you feel guilty because you've decided to make the necessary changes in your life. If you're going to get influenced by someone, it might as well be yourself—consciously, by the stuff you feed your own mind with.

3. **There's something powerful about journaling.** It's simply writing down your thoughts, ideas, and feelings on paper to understand them more clearly. Imagination is an extremely powerful method to ignite an idea; getting it on paper ignites its tangible existence in the physical realm. I could've easily continued to imagine and think about this book coming into the world, but without taking out the necessary action, the book would only reside in my head and sit dormant. It would just remain a thought. Journaling also

offers a safe space to express how you feel and provides you with a guide to keep track of your progress and growth through continual reflection. I also find it a powerful way to increase your cognitive abilities.

During my high school years, I would always be placed in the lowest maths class and struggled with numbers. Once I commenced my studies to become an electrician, I was shocked to find that the whole course was heavily based on mathematics. I felt doomed, hopeless and anxious. How was I expecting to pass such a complex curriculum? Having that 'don't give in attitude,' I went to all extremes to pass, even though I failed multiple semesters. I made it my mission to prove to myself I could do it, even after I was told to quit by several teachers. Having a persistent mindset, I would cut dozens of A4 pieces of paper in half. Write down all of the equations we had to learn, and I would stick them everywhere in my room, including the ceiling. The idea of this was to visually see these equations right before bed and first in the morning so my subconscious mind began downloading all the information. When it came to the exams, not only did I pass with flying colours, I went on to become Australia's best electrical contractor in 2021 at The Australian Business Champion Awards in front of 1,000 people at The Star, Sydney. The only limitations we have in our minds are the limitations we place on ourselves. Write down what you want so it's etched in your mind. Feel what this experience would be like. Writing it down on paper, creates a powerful weapon and bridges the gap between your imaginative faculty and your fulfilled objective. It's yours. Go get it.

3

INTUITION THROUGH DIVINE FORCES

Amid the dreaded walls of Goulburns Maximum Security Prison, a place stained with a history of violence and known as the 'killing fields' of the 70s and 80s, my entrepreneurial journey took a pivotal turn. This institution, one of Australia's oldest, was not just a facility for confinement but a ground where battles of the soul were fought and often lost. Here, amidst the eerie silence punctuated by the echoes of its dark past, I embarked on a path not just of redemption, but of divine awakening.

On a quiet New Year's Eve in 2011, I found myself, for the first time in my life, alone. In a prison cell. Lost in thought. I was majorly depressed and crippled with anxiety. Confined in a small 4m x 2m space, with only a stainless-steel toilet and a mattress a few feet away, I was left alone with my thoughts, much like Tom Hanks' character and his imaginary friend, Wilson, in the movie

Castaway. This experience taught me a crucial lesson early on: never let pride stop you from seeking help when you need it the most. It's a pivotal lesson. I learned it the hard way, but that doesn't have to be the same for you.

Before my arrest, I didn't feel quite right that night. My intuition was pushing me back. My ego and stubbornness couldn't be stopped. The signs were there, but I chose to turn a blind eye and take the path of least resistance, following through with my illegal act. The price was heavy.

During a desperate time, struggling financially, I made a decision that cost me my liberty. My arrogance blinded me to the potential consequences of my actions. My actions were catastrophic. Ironically, getting caught was a turning point for me. It was the best thing that could've happened. I wouldn't be the person I am today had I not experienced this phase of my life. At 29, having never faced legal trouble and immersed in the world of startups, I was extremely naive. My legal troubles not only ended my ventures but also left me with a mountain of debt. It also placed huge pressure on my elderly parents and family.

The younger version of me always struggled to ask for help, feeling it was a burden to others. My pride always got in the way. This kind of mindset can cause complications. Never let your pride stop you from seeking assistance, guidance, and feedback. If you have decent humans within your circle, there's no reason for them not to help, especially if you're in dire straits.

There's always someone willing to listen and help when it's necessary in your life. When the grappling feeling of anxiety or fear sets in, always remember you only feel this way because you haven't found a solution - yet. Perhaps you have found a solution; you've just failed to ask. The answers are out there, waiting for you. All of the universal energy we see around us is neither created nor destroyed. We just need to surrender and learn to tap into that force that's always within our reach.

This has been proven through science and physics, time and time again. So, if we come to the conclusion that whatever is 'here now' has always 'been here' and whatever you seek in the future is 'already here' - then why do we wrestle with fear, anxiety and doubt so much?

We need to teach (our human form) that we are infinite, spiritual beings living in a physical realm of exceptional potential. This potential can be accessed anywhere, anytime. You need to put in the work first. Taking action is a monumental step towards arriving at your desired outcome. I want to share a story with you to prove that almost every time, our answers come to us intuitively. We just need to learn how to accept them through spiritual means. If you're not spiritual, that's okay. I'm not trying to push any beliefs on you. That's your journey and decision to make. However, I can't ignore the fact that I've experienced supernatural moments. This can't be ignored and must be shared for the betterment of anyone reading this book.

Get rid of the idea that everything must be solved by you, and you alone. There are unseen forces guiding every single one of us. Every second. Every minute, of every day. Solving complex situations does not necessarily take more grit and muscle. It merely takes the ability to open up your heart and mind: and the flow commences.

When you accept the fact that there's something far greater than us here on Earth, you open up the quantum realm of possibility and your resources start to dramatically materialize through your existence. Just because you can't see something tangible, it doesn't mean the work isn't being completed behind the scenes through the unseen forces. It's not your job to know how this is being done. Your job is to ask the right questions mixed with faith. Questions like, "Who can guide me on the right path to find my answers?" or "What can I learn to get me closer to my desired outcome?" Negativity will only halt your progression.

Have an open mind and think beyond your conventional and habitual thinking. The same way of thinking you've been carrying with you your whole life, will merely get you more of the same. If you're not happy with your current circumstances, it's time to shift that paradigm. The only person that can take that leap is you.

Albert Einstein, one of the greatest scientists of all time, famously said, "Insanity is doing the same thing over and over again and expecting different results".

Nikola Tesla, arguably the greatest inventor of all time, also said, "If you want to find the secrets of the universe, think in terms of energy, frequency and vibration".

Here are two great men of the 20th century who have given priceless advice for the ages. For them to make these statements, it means that they have personally experienced something significant. Even though their teachings and wisdom have been around for decades, we often find ourselves falling back into our mundane routines. Grinding, without a purpose. Looking for a miracle to change our circumstances. We start blaming everyone else but ourselves. Stop thinking you're just a physical body and start realizing our spiritual capabilities are far more potent.

After all, our bodies are merely just temporary vessels. Our 'physical' appearance, no matter how well you look after it, will eventually give way at some point in your life. I'm not saying for you to neglect your body. In fact, exercise and training are a huge part of my life. Without it, I'd be lost. I will always endeavour to give myself the biggest opportunity possible to get to 100 years old and beyond (God willing). On the other hand, our physical bodies are ignited and lit up by an extraordinary force called the spirit. The human spirit is an unsurpassable force that fuels our drive, resilience, and passion. It is the essence of our being, transcending physical limitations and propelling us toward greatness. By tapping into the power of the human spirit, we harness an inner strength that enables us to overcome obstacles, pursue our dreams, and achieve extraordinary feats. This vital force is the engine behind our physical bodies, igniting our motivation, creativity, and perseverance. Recognizing and nurturing the human spirit is crucial, as it is the driving force that empowers us to lead purposeful and fulfilling lives.

Something else I have also found intriguing is that after a human body dies, the body weighs exactly the same straight after death. If it weighs the same, this means that the spirit driving our physical bodies is weightless yet so powerful. It's something of divine nature – from a higher realm. We all harness this power and it's all within our reach. This is why we need to rely on and feel our intuition now more than ever. With all the technology around us nowadays, it's very easy to get distracted and rely on external forces, rather than listen to our internal dialogue and feel more through our own vibrational frequency. Once you learn how to harness it, the answers start to flow much easier. Tapping into this remarkable power source is a game changer.

After my release years later, facing financial strain from delayed payments whilst completing a major project, I was reminded of past challenges. As always, I turned to prayer and stillness. Having the ability to calm the mind and block out unnecessary noise is profound. I seeked answers so I could take action. It's crucial to recognize our inner voice, a blend of intuition and divine guidance, that often points us in the right direction. A friend of mine, let's call him 'Mr T', kept coming to mind and as the day passed, my feelings got stronger and stronger. Despite my initial resistance (going back to my habitual human patterns), I felt compelled to reach out and call. Our conversation led to an immediate offer of help, reinforcing the value of true friendship and the unexpected ways help can manifest. Mr T's generosity taught me an unforgettable lesson that day. The importance of being there for others. In good times and in bad times. His words etched deeply into my mind and body. His trust and support were a beacon during a tough time. Before I could finish talking, Mr T had already offered to be my pillar of support. He didn't flinch because the trust was there. I repaid Mr T back within six weeks, His act of generosity was mind blowing. If it wasn't for him, I would've been in a very difficult situation. An experience I'll always cherish and hold close to my heart.

The essence of this story ties back to a powerful biblical principle: "Ask, and it will be given to you; seek, and you

will find; knock, and the door will be opened to you"
(Matthew 7:7-8).

It's crucial to remember that solutions are closer than
they appear. We just never take the first step to ask, therefore we don't receive. This is why we tend to go through
life constantly anxious and depressed. We place unnecessary pressure on ourselves thinking we must know all the
answers to our problems - and we must know them now.

Unwanted chaos, negativity, and toxicity will also slow
down the process and potentially block your intuitive
instincts even more. Receiving help and guidance from
infinite intelligence will never be achieved through muscle
and manpower alone. It takes an individual to understand
that consciousness and self-awareness are key to unlocking the highest gifts we all harness. You were born with it.
And it'll always be there. Unfortunately, our habitual up-
bringing, ingrained programs, and limiting beliefs—often
passed down through our parents, families, and leaders—
have dulled these vital senses, but that is about to change.

Never let ego or doubt overshadow your ability to connect
with your inner wisdom or the divine power. Remember,
even in complete isolation, we're never truly alone; a
higher force guides us. Offering light even in the darkest
and most challenging moments. Start embracing darkness
as a beautiful component in life. Doesn't a new day start in
the dark? Even the brightest and most colourful flowers

start as a small seed planted deep under the soil. Dark and moist. Once you start to change your perception, many aspects of your life will shift considerably, and the outcomes will shift in your favour.

Let this be a guide for overcoming obstacles. Be alert in recognizing the divine in our lives and the miracles that shape our path. Let's embrace the synchronicities that guide us, moving beyond coincidence to a deeper understanding of our connectedness and purpose.

From this chapter, three additional pillars emerge as guideposts for personal and professional triumph. If you can implement these three crucial pillars, they can potentially work wonders in your life.

1. **Trusting Internal Cues:** Learn to trust the powerful, subtle internal cues that guide us toward our next steps or the people who can pivot us in the right direction. It costs nothing to have faith and trust the unseen forces. It costs nothing to ask someone for help. If you're too afraid of getting rejected that's okay. Just remember, if you never asked in the first instance, it was always going to be a 'no' anyway - so if you get a hunch to call, go to a meeting, randomly get invited to an event, or a message pops into your mind to call someone - it's your cue to act. It's a huge nudge, make the effort and take charge.

2. **Recognising Shared Journeys:** Recognise that our journey is shared, and the support we need often comes from the collective wisdom and generosity of those around us. Building your network is pivotal in both your personal and professional life. When you build key relationships, integrity, and most importantly, trust, you build unshakable strength between your peers and allies. It may take up to 20 years to build a great reputation and only 20 seconds to spoil it. Always treat your peers and close allies with the utmost respect. If you say you're going to do something, do it. If they help and support you, repay the favour. Don't burn bridges because of ego or self-cockiness and never do wrong by someone for no reason. If your allies are staunch, do the same and keep them close. If you're in a position to help someone, be the person that changes their life by giving them what they need in that given moment. Individuals with a healthy conscience and strong morals will never forget these gestures. This plays a pivotal role when in search for answers because you have naturally aligned yourself with individuals who are vibrating at the same level as you. Your intuition instinctively knows where to look. Think of it as a high frequency antenna tuned to the right station.

3. **Operating at the Highest Level:** To operate at the highest level and be open to the signs and cues, you must always treat yourself as an elite athlete. Mind and body are not separate entities; they are one. If your body and mind are in great shape and you constantly work on both, they work in unison. They will be congruent, which elevates your output and potential. By having a strong and healthy body, in conjunction with a winning mindset, we operate at an optimum level by establishing unwavering clarity. The channels of unseen forces will open brightly in your life. Start trusting the stuff you cannot see. "Blessed are those who have not seen and yet believe" (John 20:29) Picture your mind as a bright beam of white light, shining from the crown of your head up to the sky as far as the eye can see. This resembles clarity and alignment. If chaos, toxicity, and negativity exist, it hinders that light with dark gloomy clouds and causes resistance. A bit like your mobile phone having no reception, disabling you from making calls. Cut out the unnecessary fogginess and blocks from your life in as many areas as possible. If you don't, this will only hinder your growth, experiences, and limit your potential. It will also hinder the connection to your higher self. Therefore, your signals will be weak. Guard it at all costs.

Always follow your intuition and internal cues. When you do, you have the potential to change your life, including those around you. You may be blessed in ways unimaginable. Prosperity is not just for personal gain but for the betterment of those within our reach. These lessons, woven through my narrative of redemption, aim to elevate you to confront your own prisons, whether they be made of iron or of the mind. As we continue through this book, remember that the keys to unlocking your full potential lie in humility, a healed heart, trusting the unseen, a growth mindset and unwavering faith. The path to greatness is paved with the stones of our past mistakes, illuminated by the light of perseverance and divine guidance.

Having the ability to give back and serve humanity is the ultimate purpose. There's no greater feeling than being able to help a fellow human and put a smile on their face. A small gesture, conversation, or even a piece of advice you shared via a one-to-one encounter, social media, or in a group setting can potentially be the catalyst for changing someone's life. True, heartfelt experiences (here on Earth) are the ultimate blessings one can bestow upon others while we're living and breathing.

Remember to always give thanks for the blessings that you have now, the blessings you've had in the past, and the blessings that are yet to come. When you practice gratitude on a daily basis, you remain grateful and grounded. It demonstrates humility, and because of this, the flow of abundance will keep returning tenfold. Gratitude is the highest vibrational level. Staying here will only accelerate your velocity in life and business.

4

THE FEELING IS PARAMOUNT

As a kid, I was very shy by nature and a huge introvert. So being thrown into my parents' take-away food shop as an 11-year-old boy taught me so much. I didn't realize it at the time, but my entrepreneurial journey began from a very young age. During those years in my parents' shop, I also experienced a monumental life lesson which I hold close to my heart. It's also a powerful weapon for every single person that reads this book, if applied correctly.

Even though I could barely see over the counter while serving our customers, these years taught me many fundamental skills such as effective communication, handling orders, preparing food, working the register, and being involved in a team environment. It also built my confidence, which I lacked leading into high school. It really got me out of my comfort zone, but that's the only way we learn and evolve as individuals. The biggest growth comes from putting yourself out there. Every Friday and Saturday night (including school holidays), I would find myself at the shop working and helping my parents. Sometimes the shop was so packed, people used to line up outside waiting to get in. Assisting my parents to lighten the load was the least I could do, seeing as though they constantly provided for me and my siblings. I never asked for money when I worked in their shops because I understood the sacrifice and pressure they had on their shoulders. I could see it in their faces, I could see the long hours they would put in on a daily basis - week in, week out. The older I got, the more I understood and respected the sacrifices they were making for their children.

Although my parents came from very little, they had a natural gift when it came to empathy and emotional intelligence. Every week, my father Michael would order large containers of lollipops along with all the other produce which was required for that week. I didn't think much of it at the time; however, it wasn't until years later that I understood the profound impact this had on someone's life. I now carry and implement this important lesson in everything I do.

My parents used to give a lollipop to every single child (with the parents' permission) as they were leaving with their food. It was a small gesture for the kids every time they would come into the shop. The smiles on the children's faces were priceless. It soon became this local tradition and every time the kids would come in, they would look for one of us in search of that lollipop.

You may not think it's a big deal. But let's fast forward 20 years later.

I was walking in my local shopping centre one day and all of a sudden, a young girl approached me out of nowhere. "Excuse me, aren't you one of the brothers that used to work in your parents' take-away shop all those years ago in Cherrybrook?" I responded "yes", and we exchanged a few words back and forth until she hit me with something special.

"I'll never forget how I used to feel when I received a lollipop from your parents. I loved coming into your shop. It made me feel so happy and special".

I was literally gobsmacked that this girl remembered these moments all those years later. This experience changed my perception towards life as it amplified the importance of human connection.

A simple 10-cent lollipop left such a profound impact and impression. It was so big and relevant that this girl remembered it two decades later. Why? How? It made me think carefully. If a small gesture can leave such a lasting impact, imagine what our words and language can do to someone's life? Especially young children. They have the ability to cut deep or spark a favourable imprint that can last for generations.

The special message in this story is simple, yet so profound: *Feeling* is the secret. Be cautious every time you interact with any individual. How will you make them feel? Will you make them feel valued? What will you say to them? How will you say it? What is your tone of voice? How do you want them to remember you? Will you compliment them? This girl remembered the feeling of love, kindness, gratitude, safety, and happiness every time she walked into our shop. That's why it's so important to leave your mark in the world by doing good deeds for others and setting a great example for humanity. I have implemented this in every single business venture I have undertaken. I can wholeheartedly say that our biggest growth and wins have come from being authentic, sincere, caring, and respectful towards everyone we interact with. If you can give in some way and not expect anything in return, it will come back to you tenfold.

I've experienced this phenomenon many times in my life. It has been proven repeatedly.

There was one time when a young man who I knew was sitting next to me at a function. He kept eyeing out one of my favourite watches I was wearing and saying how cool it was. He had this fascination with timepieces and I could tell he meticulously looked after his own as he kept polishing the watch face at every given opportunity. Towards the end of the night, I approached him and greeted him goodbye. I took off my watch and without hesitation, I gave it to him. He thought I was giving it to him just to try it on. I asked him, "Do you like it?" He was in awe and kept looking at the watch, struggling to get a word out. I told him I had been watching him during the night and noticed how much he admired his own watch by keeping it clean. "If you had this watch, would you look after it too?" I said to him. "Of course!" the young man responded. "It's yours," I told him. He was speechless and gave me the biggest bear hug. I'm not sure who was more excited, me or him. The feeling of giving back is a natural high. The chemicals that transfer throughout your body make you feel something extraordinary. It's pure bliss.

The story doesn't end there.

Fast forward three days later. I was having a coffee with a friend and owner of one of the major developments we were doing at the time near Sydney's CBD. This friend had contracted us to do all of the electrical work from the ground up. It was a big project which took us two years to complete. We were now in the final two weeks of the project, and it was coming to an end. He sat me down, and after a brief discussion, he thanked me for all my efforts. He also sprung a huge surprise on me which left me speechless. "I want to give you a $15k bonus as a gift from me. You did a great job." My response mimicked the young man a few nights earlier. I was in shock, yet I felt elevated. I told him that it wasn't necessary. He insisted and told me he wouldn't take no for an answer. After I thanked him a dozen times, I respectfully and politely accepted the offer. I said to myself, "This man's incredible," not just because of the extremely kind gesture, but the fact that he had the empathy and capacity to do something noble. Something I would remember forever. Take away the monetary value, it was the fundamental lesson that impacted me the most. He made me feel special by his words. That meant more to me than anything. It left an impact.

I told my wife Connie a few hours later. She simply smiled and told me she was waiting for something like that to happen. She just didn't know when and didn't expect it so soon after witnessing me giving away one of my favourite and most expensive watches.

See, when you give with a sincere heart, the universe tends to reward you when you least expect it. And when it does come back to you, be conscious to accept it with open arms. Give thanks and show a tonne of gratitude. Get out of the habit of rejecting the gifts and blessings that come your way. If they are heading in your direction, they're coming your way for a reason. By rejecting them, you're telling God, the universe, and the unseen forces that you don't feel worthy enough to receive them. Therefore, this creates a block and potentially restricts you from receiving more in the future. You reap what you sow. The more you sow, the more you'll reap. Your blessings are in direct proportion to what you protrude out to the world. It's a powerful weapon. Yet people are forgetting the art and power of this incredible trait and gift we all possess. Everyone has this ability to give back. It's a choice. Never have the mindset of scarcity. This is an extremely negative psychological pattern. Don't amplify more of what you don't want in your life. If you struggle with this and you feel yourself always falling back into this pattern, please start with just doing one or two great gestures every day for somebody else. Your life will shift, and you will be filled with abundance soon thereafter.

If you want to see a profound shift in your life or business, there are three important key lessons I would love for you to take away from this chapter.

1. **True Empathy Causes Elevation.** No matter where you are in life – a business owner, team leader or you're flying solo at present, one of the strongest traits you can have in your arsenal is empathy. Every time you're in an important meeting or having a difficult conversation with someone, I want you to do more 'listening' than talking. The art of listening is extremely powerful. Many of us are used to rambling on and telling the world how great we are; however, if you're good at what you do, your results will speak

volumes on their own. They will do all the talking for you. You have no idea how much information you can gather by listening to someone. Once you can master this and have the control to find the correct balance between speaking and listening, you gain the wisdom and clarity to change some- one's life. The cues will be shown to you, but you need to be fully conscious. There's a reason why God created us with two ears and one mouth. Gazing at your phone whilst you're with someone every five seconds is not going to help the cause either. It's disrespectful, and I would put it away if you can. Eliminate any distractions. If you're in someone's presence, give them your full attention. Be immersed. Be present. Be invested. People can sense if you truly care, or if you're just there to fill the time. If you don't want to meet with someone, be honest in a respectful way and decline. But if you commit to something, give it everything. When you show true empathy, you master the ability to share and understand the feelings of another. This creates a fortified bond which will then lead to trust, collaboration, and a plethora of potential business transactions for the future.

2. **The Art of Giving is Profound.** If you're a true professional, you will naturally give and expect nothing in return. You don't have to give away a watch every time you interact with someone.

Giving can be achieved in an infinite number of ways. Start with your language. Give someone a random compliment. You wouldn't believe how far this has got me in life. Your language and words have the ability to make someone feel unbelievable. You have the ability to raise someone's vibration just by smiling at them and expressing gratitude. The energy you project has the power to uplift an individual. But it also has the ability to make someone feel terrified, worthless, and rattle their confidence. If you're in a restaurant and the waiters have provided great service, tip them. Remember their names for next time. I guarantee you; you will be treated like kings and queens next time you visit them. If you provide a service, what is something extra you can provide as a free gesture to show you care and value this person or new client? People will always remember how you make them feel. If you make people feel like a million dollars every time you interact with them, they will keep coming back for more because they feel valued, respected, and know they always get more than what they pay for. This is the level you want to operate at. Part-time effort will only get you part-time results. Instead, put in the work and watch the velocity of your life explode to new heights. Start planting those seeds and watch them sprout: the laws of the universe have got your back.

3. **Balancing Technology and Human Skills:** Technology has evolved so much nowadays. It has gotten to the point that we can't keep up with all the trends, updates, and new products on the market. Over the last 20 years, it's hard to fathom how far we have come, especially with AI now revolutionising the scene and how it's changing the way we do things in almost every facet. I believe this has started to affect our people skills, especially with our youth. We live in an extremely fast-paced world and always find ourselves running and adhering to our daily routines. Our eyes are glued to a screen for most of the day, and we can't seem to function without our mobile phones. Although technology is important and an integral part of our successes, too much of one thing will start to affect certain areas of your life. Something needs to give. Some people sacrifice their health. Others are willing to lose relationships, and some are oblivious to the fact that they have lost the art of socializing. Human connection is pivotal to our survival. Not interacting with other people can lead to unhealthy habits, such as not eating properly and not getting enough sleep. In addition, loneliness can also augment stress, depression, and anxiety. I know plenty of people who get anxious at the thought of just being in a crowded environment. I see our youth struggling to hold a conversation.

I see grown adults not knowing how to effectively communicate with those closest to them. Sitting behind a screen is so much easier than facing someone face-to-face. Mastering your personal skills like communication, negotiation, problem-solving, and leadership aren't going to be achieved by mere fluke. You can't rely on generative AI, language models or search engines to give you all the answers and expect to be a pro in the space of 5 minutes. You must get your hands dirty and do the physical work to obtain a higher level of competence. Self-control leads to self-mastery. These human skills enable us to interact with our fellow brothers and sisters and give us the confidence to tackle the world head-on.

We need to be more conscious of when it's time to be on technology, and when it's time to clock off. We need to have self-control. We opt for the quick dopamine hit rather than accepting delayed gratification. Don't be fooled by the social conditioning that has potentially been placed on you. Screen-sucking on everyone's socials all day whilst lying in bed is definitely not going to get you closer to your goals. Place the focus on your journey to become better; mentally, spiritually, physically, and financially. By creating healthy habits, we can then be great role models and mentors for our youth and those around us. We can teach them the skills to be confident and proud human beings heading into life. When there's a difficult conversation, you'll be prepared. When there are trials, you'll be prepared. When you need to negotiate, you'll be prepared. You'll be prepared and confident because you have put in the work.

It's so important for everyone to have effective people skills. They are majorly relevant in today's world. Too many distractions are stripping these skills away. We can't have this. Lead by example, and if you have the ability to teach or mentor in any way possible, I urge you to do it. Your future self and the greater world will thank you later in life.

5

MASTER YOUR CRAFT

During my early days of entrepreneurship, I was obsessed with making money. At one point, it was all I thought about. Don't get me wrong, money is great. We need it to live phenomenal lives. But if money is your only driving force, it will eventually lose its spark. I made it my sole purpose, and this wasn't healthy. There was no meaning behind my transactions, and I wasn't delivering exceptional service. It was good, not great. It wasn't until a wise man told me not to obsess over money in the early stages of business. He advised me to master my craft first; then the money would flow abundantly. This way, it would bring greater meaning and impact.

At first, this advice didn't resonate with me because I was very impatient in my 20s. As I reflected on it, my father's voice echoed in my mind. He was a master of patience. My father could build and create amazing things without needing to sketch them out. He visualised everything in his mind and was exceptional with his hands. Everything he touched turned to gold. I admired his cool, calm, and collected persona. If it meant taking an extra week to build something, he would put in the effort to ensure it was perfect. For my dad, there was no substitute for quality.

That's why it bothers me nowadays that so many people want top dollar without mastering their craft. They're still novices, mediocre at best, believing that part-time effort will bring a life of glory and riches. Why is everyone in such a rush to get to the top without putting in the effort? Many people get caught up in social media, comparing themselves to others who have been in the game much longer. They become disheartened when they haven't reached their desired outcome after a short period of time.

A bodybuilder who has been training for one year won't have the same physique as one who has been training for twenty years. It just doesn't make sense. You can't compare yourself to someone with many more seasons of experience. The victories and wisdom they've gained are far greater. It's healthy to admire these people and gain wisdom if you strive for a similar vision. However, we need to learn the art of patience. Mastering your craft is essential to becoming known and making an impact within your industry. What will be your point of difference? How much work are you putting in? If you put in the same number of hours as your competition, what will set you apart?

During my time in Goulburn's maximum-security prison, I begged the correctional guards to give me work in the prison's factory. They kept declining me as I was on remand, meaning I could be moved at any time. They saw this as a liability. They wanted to teach and hire inmates who were committed and knew they would be there for long periods of time, which created stability within the complex. I lost count of how many times I got rejected. I figured my confidence was already bruised and broken—a few more hits weren't going to hurt. Even though the inmates got paid to work, I never gave up and told them I was willing to work for free just to prove that I had the skills to make a difference. After a couple of months, I suspect they got pissed and finally surrendered to my requests.

"Theodoridis, if we give you a job will you stop asking us?" one of the guards said. My response: "You bet. When can I start?" I told him. The next morning, I was up at the crack of dawn eager to start my first day. I kept low at first. Some of the working inmates were doing life sentences and were part of some serious gangland wars. So the last thing I wanted to do was put a foot wrong. I always showed respect and didn't do anything without asking.

You have to remember that some days inmates are walking on edge, knowing that they're doing 25 years and above. One small mishap had the potential to trigger someone. It was important to constantly observe and see everyone's reactions in case someone was about to lose their shit. Some of these guys looked so calm. You'd never pick they were some of the hardest inmates. They looked like just any other person. I was amazed how they remained so tame knowing they wouldn't see freedom for decades. Inner acceptance and accountability are such powerful weapons. Once you truly grasp and master this, nothing can control you. It's like finding a secret strength within yourself that no one can take away. When you embrace this power, you realise that even in the darkest times, you have the light to guide you through. It's very much like how Nelson Mandela served 26 years in prison gracefully and went on to become the President of South Africa. A remarkable story which embodies the true power of forgiveness and inner peace.

The factory within the jail was quite large. We had access to all the tools, and we made furniture for other prisons throughout the county. It made me take my mind off the barrage of shitty thoughts that were plaguing my mind at the time. I was so immersed in my work that I kept smashing out the tasks within the due time frame. "Keep loading me up," I'd say to them. They kept telling me to slow down. Slow down? Why? I asked them. If I slow down anymore, I'm going to seize up. Within a couple of weeks, I was given a pay rise. A whopping $9.50 per week as a full-time employee within the prison. This was achieved because I was *mastering my craft*. Money was not the main objective. I wanted to provide huge value so they could see my worth. People aren't stupid. They can see who has potential and who hasn't. Who's all in and who's not. For me, it wasn't about the money. It was the principle. I was willing to do whatever it took to make sure my sanity was in check. I was also learning new skills and aiming to perfect them. Getting paid as an inmate working in a maximum-security prison was a huge bonus. It came naturally after 'mastering my craft'. This taught me so much about staying humble and remembering your roots. One day you could be soaring high. Next minute you can crash and burn. This applies to all areas in life.

I have always admired elite athletes. When it comes to the debate about the greatest basketball player of all time, one name stands out in bold, unchallenged letters: Michael Jordan. MJ transcended the sport, transforming the NBA into a global phenomenon. His legacy is etched not only in the history books but in the hearts of fans worldwide. Jordan wasn't just a player; he was a force of nature, a relentless competitor whose drive for excellence was unparalleled. He constantly defied the laws of gravity.

Michael Jordan's career is a dazzling array of accolades and achievements. He led the Chicago Bulls to six NBA championships, securing his place in history with two separate three-peats from 1991-1993 and 1996-1998. Jordan's six NBA Finals MVP awards are a testament to his dominance on the biggest stage, where icons are made. His career average of 30.1 points per game, the highest in NBA history, showcases his scoring prowess. But what truly set him apart was his unyielding will to win. Yet, the road to greatness wasn't without obstacles. Early in his career, Jordan faced the mighty Detroit Pistons, who famously employed the "Jordan Rules" to thwart him. Instead of faltering, he used these setbacks as fuel, honing his skills, bulking up his physique, and sharpening his mental game. Each failure was a stepping stone, driving him to perfect his craft and find that elusive edge over his competition. His journey is a masterclass in resilience and perseverance.

Jordan's commitment to improvement was legendary. He would outwork everyone, arriving early and leaving late, always searching for ways to elevate his game. His famous quote, "I can accept failure, everyone fails at something. But I can't accept not trying," encapsulates his relentless pursuit of greatness. It wasn't just about winning; it was about being the best version of himself, every single day. Off the court, Jordan's influence was equally profound. He became a cultural icon, his Air Jordan brand redefining the sneaker industry, and his competitive spirit inspiring millions. Jordan's ability to thrive under pressure, his clutch performances, and his unwavering confidence turned him into more than a basketball player; he became a symbol of excellence and the embodiment of the American Dream.

In the books of sports history, Michael Jordan stands alone. A titan whose legacy continues to inspire future generations. His story isn't just about the championships or the scoring titles; it's about an unrelenting desire to be the best and the understanding that true greatness comes from the continuous pursuit of improvement. MJ was obsessed with winning. Although he was a master in his craft, he had a secret weapon always by his side during those glory days. That mentor and trainer was Tim Grover. Known as the trainer to the stars, Grover had a huge impact on Jordan's career. Grover wasn't just a trainer; he was a game-changer who pushed Jordan to reach new heights, both physically and mentally.

Tim Grover came into Jordan's life when he needed it most. After losing to the tough Detroit Pistons in the playoffs, Jordan needed a new edge. That's when Grover stepped in. He was a young, ambitious trainer with a different approach. He promised Jordan that he could make him stronger, faster, and more resilient. From their first meeting, it was clear that Grover's methods were unique. Jordan gave Tim an opportunity to prove himself in 30 days. Those 30 days turned into 15 years. A true testament to both men who made a mutual decision to be 'ALL IN.' Tim focused on making Jordan's body and mind bulletproof so he could dominate the court.

Grover's training was intense and tailored specifically for Jordan. He created workouts that addressed Jordan's weaknesses and enhanced his strengths. With Grover's help, Jordan transformed his body. He added muscle to withstand the physical play of the Pistons and improved his agility and endurance to stay at his best all season long. Grover's philosophy was simple: there's always room to get better, no matter how good you are.

But Grover's impact wasn't just physical. He taught Jordan to focus and push himself relentlessly. Grover introduced the idea of the "0.01%," meaning that even the smallest improvements could make a big difference. This idea clicked with Jordan, driving him to always strive for that extra edge. Together, they formed a partnership based on trust and hard work. The results speak for themselves. With Grover's training, Jordan secured six NBA championship rings. His body became stronger, his endurance unmatched, and his ability to perform under pressure legendary. Grover's influence was key to Jordan's success, especially in the biggest moments of his career. Beyond the championships and accolades, Grover's real legacy is the mental toughness he helped Jordan develop. He taught Jordan to love the grind, to be comfortable being uncomfortable, and to always push for more. This relentless drive became a key part of Jordan's greatness and a testament to Grover's impact.

In Michael Jordan's story, Tim Grover is the behind-the-scenes architect of his greatness. His innovative training and mental strategies helped shape Jordan into not just the best player of his time, but perhaps the best of all time. Grover's legacy lives on in every championship ring, every clutch moment, and every highlight. He's a reminder that behind every great athlete is a mentor who pushed them to be their best.

I had the ultimate pleasure of being personally mentored by Tim Grover. Every week for two months, we gathered on a live call to listen to Tim's teachings, led by his business partner and co-author Shari Wenk, an amazing woman. People from all over the world joined. It was an experience I'll always cherish. It was the last time Tim and Shari held these live coaching sessions as a group. Being in the presence of greatness is not something you get to experience every day. These moments are life-changing and make you realise why the best of the best always want more—they're never satisfied.

They say that "proximity is power." I believe this, but I'd like to go one step further by saying, "proximity utilised is power."

What do I mean by this?

Just because you surround yourself with great individuals doesn't mean your successes will manifest on their own.

Don't wait for someone to come and save you or give you a step-by-step guide on what to do. You can be trained or mentored, but there will be countless instances where you need to step into the arena, ready for battle. Be the one who saves yourself. It's okay to have a coach and be part of a great support group, but if you're not willing to put in the work, you're not only fooling yourself; you're also wasting everybody's time. As Tim says, "Are you interested or obsessed?" There's a big difference when you fully commit to something and strive for great things in your life, compared to mediocre efforts. Tim also shared with us that "Interested people watch obsessed people change the world". Interested people treat their chosen path as a hobby, they're not all in. Don't be one of these people. Especially if you're striving for huge results - make an impact by investing in the work.

Once you commit and decide to go all in, you'll soon discover that people will try to talk you down and troll you. They'll try to talk you out of things and call you names. They'll tell you you've changed. They will also be the ones who say they're not interested in what you're doing yet secretly keep a close eye on you, holding their breath, waiting for you to fall. Don't waste time on people like this. It's wasted energy. Instead, make a promise to yourself that you'll see it through, whatever endeavour you're chasing. Prove to yourself that you can do anything you put your mind to. Start creating the desired picture in your mind and begin connecting the dots toward your obsession. Your final destination. Learn everything you can from your mentors and individuals who can elevate you. Listen to them. Ask questions. Then implement everything you have learned. Utilise the information and wisdom you have gathered. Don't let it sit dormant and place it on a shelf to collect dust. This will give you nothing in return.

When you decide to master your craft, these are the three key ingredients I recommend you follow and implement. They are profound and powerful which can elevate you to exceptional heights.

1. **Get Comfortable Saying No.** To master your craft and be the best, you need a schedule. If you want to achieve great things, you can't expect to attend every networking event, sporting event, and social event and still fit in all your mundane tasks. Seriously, what time will be left for your vision? When will you put in the work? Once you have a schedule, don't let yourself be pulled away every time something comes up. It will affect your performance and progression. I understand everyone has different obligations, and kids can take up a large portion of your time. But that doesn't mean you can't still achieve and do exceptional things. Saying no shows inner strength and discipline. It also sets boundaries with people who no longer serve you and don't align with

your beliefs. Most people may not understand you, that's okay. Don't fall for the peer pressure around you. Be more selfish and do the things you want to do. If you don't create your own schedule, someone will create one for you, and that's not healthy. Aren't you deserving of dreaming about conquering something great? You will be constantly tested in this area, and it's up to you to decide where to give your precious time. I was heavily criticised when I pulled away from many things in my life. I was totally comfortable with my decision and had no regrets. Because I knew if I didn't, the price of regret would be much higher. Start orchestrating your life. Make it work for you, not against you. Be cautious with your time; there are energy leeches everywhere. Start getting comfortable pressing the delete button. Saying no is a strength, not a weakness.

2. **Embrace the Willingness to Learn and Adapt.** To be the best, you have to have a deep willingness to constantly learn new things. Don't be a one-hit wonder. Just because you win some trophies, receive some acknowledgments, or secure a million-dollar deal, it doesn't mean it's your cue to slacken off and take your foot off the pedal. When you find yourself at the top of your game, everyone wants your position. You'll be scrutinised. People will want to see you fall.

They'll talk behind your back and do whatever it takes to dethrone you and push you to the bottom. It doesn't get easier when you master your craft and become the best. It becomes insanely harder. Scaling to the next level will require a new set of skills. Your arsenal will need an upgrade. You'll find last year's artillery is outdated and simply won't cut it. Winning takes discipline and a deep yearning for sacrifice, self-belief, and commitment. Winning needs all of you. It will test you over and over to see how badly you want it. When you have the enthusiasm to thrive and learn, not only do you develop new skills, but it also gives you the ultimate chance of survival and to stay at the top. If you're comfortable being the same as most people, that's fine. It's your choice. This is for the individuals who want to be prolific in their chosen profession. It's for those who want to make some noise and shake things up. Prolific individuals grind with a deep purpose. This is embedded within their hearts and minds. Mediocre people who grind with no meaning and purpose give up easily. They continuously change to new things. Their grinding never takes shape. They're the same individuals who tell you 'It's the journey that counts,' nothing else. How can you truly enjoy the journey when you don't have a destination and a clear vision? People who strive to be the best versions of themselves cut away the unessentials. They block out the noise and turn up every day. They can visualise how their life will be in the future. They also have the tenacity to stay in the game for the long haul. After many seasons, their grinding pays off. It takes the shape they had always envisioned. This is achieved by having a growth mindset and the relentless hunger to learn and develop new skills. We should all take note of Michael Jordan's story. Although he was the best, he sought for more. He didn't let his own ego or pride get in the way of learning—even though he was at the top. As a result, it propelled him to exponential heights. The rest is history.

3. **Through reflection and introspection, you'll find your true direction.** You'll have days when you feel no progress has been made. That's okay. It's important to understand that even on the days you don't think you're making progress; you are. Every night before going to bed, it's pivotal to sit and reflect on the day. What did I accomplish? Who did I speak to? Did I leave an impact? Did I turn up to train? Did I learn something new? You'll be surprised how many things will come to mind. When they do, take them and deposit them in your 'reflection bank account' - you've just made a conscious deposit on your daily wins. After a week, a month, a year; these small wins which you have accumulated over the course of

many months, become extraordinary. It becomes a mountain of triumphs. Each takes you one step closer to your desired destination. Most individuals underestimate how much they can accomplish in six months, let alone one year. Remember what I said earlier in this book? 'The only limitations we have are the ones we place in our own minds.' Next time you make an allowance for how long something should take to achieve; I want you to halve it. We tend to set the date so far ahead to play it safe. It's more comfortable. It gives us more time.

Every level of success will get harder and harder. Staying the same simply won't be good enough. You should always strive to become better every single day, week, and month. After every birthday, I always reflect on the last twelve months. I ask myself: 'Have I elevated myself?' 'Am I wiser?' 'Is this the last one?' 'How many more birthdays do I have left here on earth?' It's imperative we strive to enhance ourselves and be fully aware that the hourglass is ticking. It rests for no one.

Ever since my father passed away in my arms in December 2021, it changed my life. Watching a soul leave someone's body is a deep spiritual moment that one should cherish forever. It shakes you to the core and makes you realise that our time here on earth is extremely limited. It's precious. If you ever have the chance to experience this with a loved one, I highly recommend it. It can have a profound impact on your life.

I often picture myself lying on a bed before my last moments here on earth, just like my father, asking myself: 'Am I satisfied?' and 'Have I given it everything?' I want no regrets in my life. That's why I strive to accomplish crazy stuff. I want to leave no stone unturned. I believe I would be doing a great injustice to myself if I never reached my full potential. Don't waste your time on things that don't bring you fulfilment and are not congruent with your higher purpose. By mastering your craft, you will generate abundance, and this will have a profound effect on your life and for those closest to you.

Mastery is about continuously honing your skills, expanding your knowledge, and pushing your limits. It's about having the courage to say no to distractions and the humility to always be a student. It's about reflecting on your progress and celebrating your small wins while keeping your eyes on the bigger prize. Mastering your craft is the gateway to living a life of purpose and fulfillment. It's the secret to turning your dreams into reality and leaving a legacy. So, commit to the journey, embrace the challenges, and dedicate yourself to becoming the best version of yourself. You have the power to create something extraordinary. Don't settle for anything less.

6

REWRITE THE SCRIPT

Towards the end of my time in Goulburn's Maximum Security Prison, I forged a close bond with a few of the islander inmates. Their yard used to back onto our yard, and we would also share the oval with them once a week. The oval at Goulburn was something else. Even though this was an eerie prison, the oval gave me peace and a sense of normality. As you walked through the gates, the oval was positioned on the lower bowl of the complex. This allowed you to see over the huge walls of the prison. You could see civilians driving their cars along the road. I often wished I could turn back time and be one of these people. I forgot how precious our liberty is. I took it for granted and this was a stark reminder to wake the fuck up! My fate was yet to be determined, and I had no idea how long I'd be behind these walls. The oval was one of my outlets. Rain, hail, or shine—I would run there at any given opportunity. One time in the torrential rain, I was the only one jogging around the oval. I could barely see in front of me. The screws (name for the correctional guards) kept telling me to get off the oval through the PA system. I ignored them. What's the worst that could happen to me? Throw me in prison? Fuck that, I told myself. I kept running. Everyone thought I was crazy, especially during winter as it was freezing cold.

I only got to use the oval once a week; I didn't care what conditions faced me. I was going to make it count, especially if it was going to help my sanity. One of Charlie Chaplin's most famous quotes was: "I always like walking in the rain, so no one can see me crying." Although running gave me the daily dose of healthy endorphins, I also shed plenty of tears in the rain. It was my outlet to release my emotions and disguise the pain.

There was word from my legal team that I was soon to be moved so I could attend court in Sydney for my sentencing. As I prepared to leave, I told one of the islander boys that I could be leaving at any given moment. One Sunday, just before my one-hour visit with my family, the bell rang for muster. This islander inmate, with whom I had forged a close bond with, called me over to the fence that divided both yards and passed me something wrapped in newspaper. I didn't know what it was at the time, but he went on to say: "This gift is special to me, but I want you to have it. It'll give you strength." I took the parcel and thanked him. By the time this occurred, we were both late in getting into the line for muster, and this caused a red flag without me even being aware.

Muster time had to be quick. It almost felt like a herd of sheep being lined up for slaughter. You had to know your place in the queue and stand in alphabetical order. As the guards yelled out your surname, you had to respond with a loud 'yes' and make your way to your cell. This enabled a quick transition. Efficiency was paramount with the guards. If you put a foot wrong or showed any signs of disrespect, they'd make you pay for it in some way.

As my name got called out, one of the intel guards grabbed me and pulled me out of the line. "Come with us," he said. "What the fuck is going on?" I asked myself. I was oblivious to what I had done. Another five guards followed, and soon they formed a circle and took me into the main building, placing me in a holding cell. All the guards came in. At this stage, I started to freak out. I had no idea why I was ostracized. As all of them were standing around me, the main screw asked me, "What the fuck did you receive through the fence?" he demanded. "I don't know," I responded. This infuriated all of them, especially the main guard. He thought I was being a smart ass. My response was the truth; however, they were not buying any of it. "What the fuck is in your bag, dickhead?" "I don't know," I responded again. This tipped the screw over the edge. He literally came so close to my face, his nose was touching mine. He then went on a barrage of abuse and called me every name you could think of. It was an intense face-off mixed with an array of spit. He went on to say I had one more chance to admit what was in the bag; otherwise, if they found any contraband, I could be facing more jail time. This would have been catastrophic.

The next phase of sequences was unrelenting. The guards picked up my bag and tipped it upside down. Everything came out in a heap of mess, including the wrapped parcel I had received moments earlier. The screws made me take off all my clothes, including my underwear. They made me spread my legs to ensure I wasn't hiding any drugs in any foreign places. Now, I was butt naked with six guards surrounding me. I still had no idea what was in the parcel. I'd never felt so humiliated, yet at this point, I was so numb and broken. Anything they did to me couldn't break me anymore. They kept pushing me to get a response. "You've got one more chance, fuckwit. What's in the parcel?" I didn't take the bait, and at this point, I gave him one word: "Nothing." I had the ultimate faith that whatever was in that parcel was good, and nothing sinister.

I said very little during the whole ordeal, and this enraged every single one of them. They finally made me open the parcel. After six layers of newspaper, the contents finally surfaced. It was an icon of Jesus Christ - a special gift that I still have to this day. In the end, the guards found nothing. Rightly so because I had nothing to begin with. They went on to tell me that contraband is a big problem within the prison complex, and they assumed I was a runner, distributing parcels within the prison. "Are you

VELOCITY

fucking serious?" I told myself. My fate is in limbo. Do you really think I would do something stupid again to jeopardise my freedom even more? No way. I copped a barrage of abuse and humiliation from the screws that day. But I received it like a champ. I didn't flinch. I didn't give them any opportunity to reprimand me even more. My emotions didn't get the better of me. Like I mentioned earlier in this book: When you control your emotions, you control the outcome.

The funny part about this experience was: if they thought I had something, why not just grab the parcel off me and open it themselves? They would have found out very quickly it was nothing. I concluded it must have been a slow day in the office for them. It was just an excuse to flex their muscles and stamp their authority with an inmate. The funny part is that the next day in muster, the same guard nodded his head at me as I walked past. As if to say: 'You passed the test', well done. It caught me by surprise, but I respectfully nodded back, reaffirming the ordeal didn't faze me as much as he'd expected it to.

At this point in my life, I was broken, and I didn't even know it. I may have been hiding it well, but I felt like my life had been smashed into thousands of pieces, all of which were now scattered on the floor. Where does the healing process start when you find yourself in this position? At the bottom of the pit. Broken and lost. The alluring part of life is that we all have the opportunity to

- 72 -

grab the pen and rewrite the script. Our current condition is never our conclusion. Never let your story restrict you from moving forward and making a positive impact in someone's life. Often, people are scared to share their story and think it's a weakness. In fact, I would go as far as to say it's your biggest strength. It becomes a powerful weapon that can impact many lives. Never be scared to share your narrative with the world. Your journey is part of the story. Without a story, it doesn't make the journey memorable. It doesn't leave a mark—your mark. By having a story, it makes you unique. It shifts you to a higher alignment and shapes you into a totally different individual. The next three points from this chapter literally transformed my life. I really struggle to find the words to describe how important they are. Follow these to build a fortress within yourself and to have the capability of writing the script you've always wanted. Become the author of your own life.

1. When you fall, don't rush to get back up . When I was incarcerated, people constantly told to get back up immediately and put it all behind me. Things were moving so fast that I couldn't comprehend what was going on. It was way too much information to process. A million things were going through my mind and I was definitely not thinking straight. I was given many opportunities to take a heap of medication to suppress the pain. I refused. Whenever you go through a hard experience, embrace the moment and fully accept the outcome for what it is.

Stay down for a little bit and understand how you got into this position. What actions got you there? What have you learned through the experience? By allowing yourself to process the situation properly, you gain a deep understanding of the lessons being displayed for you. You also get to feel every emotion of the whole trial - and this is powerful. If you get back up straight away, what have you felt? What did you learn? You've given yourself no time to fully embrace the gold nuggets that are in front of you. You'll know when it's time to rise. Believe me, when you do, you'll never be the same person ever again. Don't rush the process, but at the same time, don't be the one who doesn't rise at all. The biggest gifts are wrapped up in the biggest rifts. Never blind yourself from the opportunity to learn and evolve. When I decided to rise, it hurt. But at the same time, I knew the advantages it would bring me. It amplified my mindset to heights I didn't think were possible. Now, when something difficult arises in my life, I rise to any challenge and know it's an opportunity to unleash my inner strength and grow beyond my limits. Every difficult moment is another layer added to your armour.

2. Remember those broken pieces scattered across the floor? Among them will be some large gold nuggets. They will become the pieces that build your resilience and tenacity. Once you decide to rise and face the world again, you have the opportunity to grab all the pieces you want to add to your artillery. You put them all back together. Your way. You also have the opportunity to leave the unwanted pieces behind. These are the ones that don't serve you anymore. They are the pieces that weigh you down. Guilt, shame, embarrassment and trauma have the ability to drag you into the abyss and stop you from reaching your maximum output. Your velocity will never reach full speed and gain momentum if you decide to drag them along. Extra baggage will only burn more fuel. You want to use this as fuel in areas that align with your higher purpose, in conjunction with becoming the optimum version of yourself. You must have a clear intention where this energy will be directed and used. Just like your unwanted thoughts, when you start to eliminate the unessentials from your life, you become extremely clear about who you are. You have set the standard. Now the gold pieces will shine ever so brightly as you progress through life.

3. When you decide to grab the pen to rewrite your script, make it count. Easy challenges give you fake rewards, whereas colossal challenges get you firing on all cylinders. They give you unbelievable results that can define your life. The butterflies start to turn. The challenge is so great that it has the potential to make you quit. It's constantly asking you: 'Do you really want it?' Or 'Are you a pretender?' It will expose you. That's when you know you're on the right track. If you were told that you had no limitations, with no glass ceiling - how far would you go with your imagination? What would you strive for? It's amazing how our core beliefs restrict us from reaching these heights. They rob us of our true potential and what we can truly achieve. Stop letting your negative thinking get in the way. Less thinking with more action will give you so much more compared to more thinking with less action. Start using your potent human faculties like we discussed in **Chapter 2:** *SUSPEND LIMITATIONS & CHANGE YOUR LANGUAGE.* Your inner wisdom is there to serve you, not work against you.

In order to rewrite a remarkable script, you must embrace the power of your instincts. Just as every animal innately knows its role from the moment of birth, humans possess an even more profound faculty. If animals can navigate their world through instinct alone, imagine the vast potential within you. Humans have a tremendous power to feel and sense the world around them, to tap into an inner wisdom that guides their path. Embrace this power, trust your instincts, and let them lead you to a life of purpose and fulfillment. By doing so, you will unlock a higher level of awareness and elevate your existence to heights you never thought possible. Never block these senses; they have the ability to propel you on the right path. Observe. Feel. Act. If you don't follow your instinct and do what you truly were destined to do in your life, you will always have a feeling of guilt, anger, and stress. Stress is pressure and unfulfillment that you decided not to deal with. Don't keep suppressing it. Start making your script count. If you settle for less, you're only cheating yourself – and I don't want that for you or anyone else reading this book. Every heartbeat that passes by is one less heartbeat you have here on this earth. You are born to be extraordinary - go hard.

7

GET COMFORTABLE FEELING UNCOMFORTABLE

Taking a quantum leap is a bold act of faith. It's thrilling, yet daunting. You will encounter many instances of turbulence. You must relinquish a sense of security, navigate through a fog of uncertainty, and tackle challenges that are starkly different from anything you've faced. You'll likely encounter failure and perhaps even criticism from those who've supported you before. But discomfort is a promising sign. It signals that you're venturing into territory that's truly worthy of your potential. The greatest risks are those that make your heart race — the ones you haven't conquered yet. A sense of ease suggests stagnation, not growth. You're not just aiming for incremental improvements but rather, a radical transformation.

In order to get what you want; you're going to have to do things you've never done. You will experience terrain you've never faced before. Your mind and faith will be stretched to the brink. It's uncharted territory. New perceptions are formed inside of you, when you have mastered the art of feeling uncomfortable. This is when true comfort begins. The common thresholds that were once embedded in you have now begun to perish. At first, you might be terrified of stepping into something new, setting big goals, or having a vision that seems unrealistic. However, it's not your problem to worry about how you're going to get there. The most important decision you can ever make is taking the first step: action. The rest will flow. Just like a freshly planted seed, it doesn't stress about how it's going to grow and push its way through the ground. Nature takes its course. It happens at the correct time. In the correct way.

As you progress along, you will understand that each day is a positive and incremental step towards the desired outcome. You unravel the puzzle as you progress. The right people come into your life at the right time. Everything starts aligning because you're vibrating at a higher level. You start attracting the right pieces. One by one, they start to form and manifest into the desired outcomes you always wanted. The pieces were always in you. They were just waiting for you to have the inner self-belief and confidence to make the leap. Not just any leap. A quantum leap. It's a leap so big that it makes your stomach turn with butterflies and gives you goosebumps. As you navigate through uncharted territory, facing challenges that are entirely new to you, imagine the familiar safety net of past

behaviours stretching thin as you push against its boundaries. There might be moments when it feels like everything is spiralling out of control. The instinct might be to
cling tightly to what's known, but the key to advancement
lies in your ability to trust and let go. Embrace the concept
of release. If you're ready to make the jump, you must first
learn to loosen your grip. Feeling uneasy? That's normal
and an integral part of the transformation. When you
commit to a quantum leap, you don't just ride the wave —
you surrender to it, controlling your path only by setting
clear intentions, persistently pursuing your goals, and
learning from every stumble along the way. You will have
the 'good' advocate on your right shoulder saying "you
can do anything," "go for it," "I believe in you," and "It's
your time to shine." Then you'll have the 'bad' advocate
on your left shoulder spitting out garbage like, "you can't
do that," "who do you think you are?" "you're crazy," "It's
never been done before," and "You're not good enough."
For the person reading this book right now, I'm here to
tell you firsthand that "YOU CAN" and "YOU WILL." I
believe in you more than anything. Never let anyone tell
you otherwise and never self-sabotage the beautiful mind
and body our creator has given you. You might not know
what your purpose in life is right now, but I can guarantee
you one very important fact: God has put you here for
many reasons, not just to fill up the seasons.

Those reasons will come to fruition the more you put
yourself out of your comfort zone and the ability to let go.

It's there where the biggest growth is crystallised. It's when the biggest answers are delivered. All the tests, trials, and tribulations are all part of the script. Your script. These moments will forever shape and mould you. Everything that happens in your life is happening to you and for you. The right answers and divine timing will only occur when you're finally ready to receive them. If God has the ability to create the heavens and the earth and all things that exist in seven days, do you think God doesn't know what's best for you and the correct timing they should occur? Do you think God has limitations on what can be produced for you? Look, I'm not trying to push any beliefs onto you. I respect all denominations. It's your life and you're entitled to believe what you feel comfortable with. However, I've experienced way too many miracles in my life to call them mere coincidences. When I sit back and think of some, they blow my mind with the impeccable timing with which they occurred.

Manifesting your desired outcome will not come from positive thinking alone, although this is a pivotal part of the process. You must make the brave and conscious decision to put two feet on the bus. Having one foot on, and one foot off will confuse the process and cause unnecessary procrastination. Once you have burning desire to get what you want, you have to make the conscious decision to go all in.

But Rob, what if I fail? I'm glad you asked this question.

Remember how we discussed the 'what if's' in Chapter 1? I guarantee you could come up with another 1000 'what if's' and make every excuse known to man why it won't work. Why not change your perception and think of all the 'what if's' that can go right? And if you do fall hard, it's going to be the most liberating experience you've ever had. You will build your wisdom, resilience, and tenacity, and it will heighten your gratitude which is one of the most powerful vibrational frequencies you can be at as a human.

Gratitude is transformative. When you're grateful, you acknowledge the good in your life, even amid challenges. This shifts your focus from scarcity to abundance, from failure to growth. Operating at a high vibrational frequency of gratitude not only enhances your well-being but also attracts positive experiences into your life. It's like tuning into the clearest, most uplifting radio station, broadcasting positivity and possibilities.

So, instead of fearing failure, embrace it as a stepping stone to greater wisdom and strength. Each stumble is a lesson, each setback an opportunity to rise stronger. Let gratitude elevate your journey, and you'll find that even in failure, there's profound growth and a path to success.

Failure is an integral part of life. We need to harness it and not treat it as something that's forbidden. I'm not saying to repeat the same failures and be reckless in your deci-

sion-making throughout life. But you need to comprehend that trials are all part of the process and it's totally
normal to have temporary seasons of defeat. When you
come back from every 'no', 'rejection' or 'failure' - you're
never the same person. Always remember, you'll find
many blessings in every lesson. Failure is on the opposite
spectrum of success. You might not be there now, but the
tide will turn in your favour once you decide to flip the
switch and show up every single day. It's inevitable. Never
shy away from the hard conversations that need to be
addressed. Most of the time, these conversations will be
with yourself. You can try and fake it with others, but you
can't hide from your own reflection and your own truths.
It follows you everywhere. Face it, embrace it, and use it
as rocket fuel. Harness the power that's embedded deep
within you. It's fuel that can last a lifetime if you harness
it the correct way. It has the potential for exponential
growth. It takes a special individual to break negative
generational cycles and beliefs. When you do, people that
were once your friends will start to distance themselves
from you and may call you weird, troll you, and try to
bring you down with their pessimism and narcissistic
behaviour. Don't be fooled by the noise and destructive
chaos that will come your way. It'll feel like the world is
against you. The pressure will feel unbearable because
you've finally dared to do something bold, courageous,
and totally against the perceived limitations you once
had.

As we touched upon in **Chapter 5: *MASTER YOUR CRAFT***, I had the privilege of being mentored by Tim Grover, one of the best trainers on this planet, alongside Shari Wenk, who is Tim's co-author for "WINNING" (New York Times Best Seller) and "RELENTLESS"

Tim Grover is an icon in his field of mastery, and his results speak volumes. Tim was the personal trainer for the great Michael Jordan and the late Kobe Bryant for many years during their careers. He has seen a thing or two when it comes to stepping out of your comfort zone, being relentless, and winning championships at the highest level. One thing that Tim taught us during our live sessions as that 'pressure is a privilege'. Never let an opportunity pass when pressure is involved. Why? These moments in life don't come often. The more you turn your back on these opportunities, the more you weaken your mind, resiliency, and spirit. Most importantly, it gives you the opportunity to prove you can accomplish something truly special. You'll find that some of the most beautiful natural phenomena on the planet are produced through pressure. Take diamonds as an example. Through intense temperatures and huge pressure under the earth's core, atoms and carbon crystallise to form sparkling diamonds. By putting yourself out there, in the heat, mixed with pressure, not only are you practising the art of getting uncomfortable, but you're also giving yourself an opportunity to shine. Through my personal experiences, these are the three most important factors to get you to a level where you become unstoppable, and push through those mental barriers to optimize your velocity.

1. **Get out your journal or a piece of paper.** I want you to draw a horizontal line across the page. Let's refer to this as the 'line of life'. On the far left, write 0 (birth) and on the far right, write 83 (death). I'm basing this figure on the most current statistic in Australia at the time of writing this book. I'm detailing this purely as an example, and I truly pray that anyone reading this book surpasses this age and reaches 100 and beyond, just like I intend to. Now, break the horizontal line into three equal parts by drawing vertical lines representing approximately 27 years each (give or take). Determine where you fit on this horizontal graph with your current age. Keep in mind that one-third of our lives are spent in bed sleeping. Also, remember that as we age, we lose mobility, flexibility, and our bodies naturally age compared to when we are in our 20s, 30s, and 40s. You start to get a good impression of how short life is and how important it is to act and take the leap of faith you've always wanted. Don't wait for that 'perfect moment.' The perfect moment for you is now. In that same journal, I want you to write down everything you're grateful for in your life right now. This makes you realize the true blessings you

have, such as health, family, and anything else that exudes abundance. It will automatically make you feel blessed and alter your physiology. Once you're finished, write down a list of goals, things that you really want to experience in this life. Is it happiness? True love? Financial freedom? Traveling the world? Becoming a professional athlete? Writing your own book or starting a business? If you want something badly enough, you'll have one that stands out from the rest. I recommend starting with one and focusing all your energy on this item to get maximum output. Instead of having 10 items and scattering your energy across all 10 desired outcomes, being laser-focused on one item at a time will give you maximum growth. Next, find three people who have mastered what you want. Narrow it down to one individual that you feel resonates with you the best. Reach out to this person, build rapport with them, and even consider doing some type of coaching with them. Your own self-development is the best investment you'll ever make. Nobody can take that away from you. It's yours for life. By learning from the best, you get information that others normally wouldn't. The biggest advantage is that you can significantly time collapse the period it would take you to learn the desired skills. Therefore, you potentially reach your desired outcome much faster. This can shave years off your journey and save you a ton of money. Indeed, time is our most precious commodity. Constantly observe and protect where your time is being allocated and use the 'line of life' as a daily reflection to remind you. Don't give yourself cheaply to everyone.

2. **Look to do something uncomfortable every day.** You might think I'm extreme but hear me out. I'm not saying to run a marathon every day of the week. Instead, do something small to start priming your mind that you're not willing to take a backward step once the voices start yelling, 'No,' 'It's too cold,' 'It's too painful,' 'I'll save it for tomorrow.' Tomorrow might never come. Don't fall for the trap of always saying no to your inner dialogue. Stop cheating yourself. You're letting your emotions overrule your mind. It must be the other way around. Your mind must be stronger than your feelings. Start with small, incremental steps. This has profound effects and pushes you that little bit further each time you commit. Make the extra five calls per day, get up a little earlier every morning to train, or even get rid of a habit that's impeding your growth or taking up too much of your time. As I mentioned earlier in the book, working inside the prison provided me with the tools to elevate my mindset

- even during the most difficult moments. Every morning, the guards would open our heavy cast iron doors, kick in our milk carton, and give us a 10-minute wake-up call at 5 am. That 10 minutes gave us time to quickly eat and get ready. There were hundreds of times I didn't feel like waking up, especially in the freezing cold, compounded with the depression and anxiety I was feeling at the time. I pushed myself to new extremes, limits I never knew existed until then. Although I was blinded at the time, these were the moments that gave me the mental tenacity I have today. I never let my emotions take over my whole body. This was achieved by doing hard stuff regularly. It fortifies the mind, and you become a beacon and role model for others. Always remember, growth is rarely forged when you live or stay in a state of comfort.

3. **Pick one or two close allies or even a mentor that you trust and who has your back.** Share what you want to achieve and ask for their unbiased advice. This can potentially steer you in the right direction and help you take the right steps. By doing so, they may be able to assist you and give you a different perspective on the situation. When you decide to commit, they will hold you accountable for seeing it through because now you've made it public to your peers. This gives

you that psychological push to see it through because you're not the only one who knows about it. Your peers know about it and are now watching your progress. You don't want to be known for starting things and not seeing them through. To be truly honest, if you want something badly enough, you'll do whatever it takes, including getting uncomfortable often. The only person you really need to hold accountable is YOU. It all starts within. You are the fuel. However, if you need some guidance in the beginning, start with this. Nothing else should matter when you decide to make a life-changing decision. This includes blocking out the external noise and criticism that comes with it.

8

PRICE FOR PROFIT

We're living in an age where competition is fierce. It seems as though every industry is saturated, and everyone is trying to make the loudest noise to gain attention. We go above and beyond to be heard and pitch until the cows come home. We spend thousands of dollars on marketing, ads, and fancy websites, and attend the biggest networking events hoping to develop key relationships. The question is, have you priced for profit or are you a commodity?

Revenue is the oxygen for any business. If the business can't breathe freely and have a healthy net profit margin, it will stay afloat for a short period of time until it suffocates and succumbs to a premature death.

Let me explain. I've been working in the service and construction industry for almost 23 years and have learnt a thing or two when it comes to pricing and knowing your numbers. Many individuals who want to go into business never sit down and work out their running costs and overheads before heading into the arena of entrepreneurship. Most individuals simply base their fee on the 'perceived industry standard'. This is dangerous territory. You can't guess your fees just because Bob down the road is doing the same. Firstly, how on earth do you know if Bob's business model is feasible? How do you know if he's making a healthy net profit? You should never compare yourself with someone else's business. That's a big error.

So many mistake gross revenue with net profit. This is not the same. Just because you turnover $1 million per annum (as an example), this doesn't mean you take home $1 million dollars. Once you factor in running costs, staff wages, taxes, and all other overheads that are associated with your business, this can turn a very big revenue number into a very small or non-existent profit.

Do you think it's a coincidence that so many companies have gone into liquidation, receivership, or administration after the effects of the infamous global pandemic? Over the last couple of years, this has left a catastrophic trail of destruction, and the aftermath will continue for some time. These challenges have notably been linked to rising labour and material costs, supply chain disruptions, and changes in consumer demand.

Once your net profit margin is slim to begin with, it's extremely difficult to bounce back and rely on a healthy reserve stack to get you through tough times: because there is none. You'll find yourself constantly chasing your tail and relying on a magical unicorn to appear and solve all your financial woes. The biggest trap people fall into is not making allowances for their own taxes and paying these on time. This is a huge dilemma, especially if you have tapped into these funds to keep your business operating. I have been through this, so I have every right to talk and give advice on this topic. If you keep falling into this trap, you can find yourself operating without the cashflow to survive, which can have so many repercussions, especially if you have staff.

Even though you need a phenomenal accounting team in your corner, you need to take full control and accountability of your finances and know your numbers better than anyone else. Spend time every week analysing and assessing what's working and what's not working. You should be working closely with your accounting team on a regular basis and seek advice if something seems foreign. Be the one who asks a million questions and never let your ego or pride get in the way of learning something new. There's a reason why you've hired the right professionals to join your team. They are there to serve, protect, and give the right advice in every aspect of your finances.

Gross revenue feeds the ego, whereas a healthy net profit feeds your lifestyle. I'm sure everybody reading this book wants to live a great, satisfying, and fulfilling lifestyle. Wouldn't you? Having the ability to do great things with your money and wealth gives you some of the best experiences life can offer. You can help your kids, family, and those closest to you. It also gives you the ability to give to those who are less fortunate. I've found throughout my life that some of the best feelings I have ever experienced are the ones where I can make someone smile because I've been able to help. You don't need money to have the ability to make someone smile, however, when you have a shit load of it, it makes life easier and less stressful.

Make sure you're charging accordingly to ensure a healthy margin every quarter. If you leave it to guesswork, you'll essentially become a commodity to society because they are only prepared to pay 'x' amount of dollars based on what they see as the perceived industry standard 'going rate'. You don't want to be competing for clients like this because it becomes a race to the bottom. You need to work out your numbers and set the tone early on what 'YOU' want to earn. Never let others dictate your worth. Especially if you have put in the necessary training and have the specialised skills and social proof to back you. Individuals who lower your worth are not worth the energy and certainly don't respect your time.

Why on earth would you put yourself through all that responsibility, stress, pressure, and sacrifice if you're making next to nothing, if any profit at all? Are you in business because someone told you it was a good idea? Or because your best friend started a business and you thought it'd be great to start one too? Earning a healthy net profit is the oxygen supply for any business. You can only cut the air supply for a short period of time. Once you suffocate: It's game over. This is crucial and a non-negotiable if you want to sustain the longevity of a profitable business and go the distance.

During my last few years as an electrician, I started to despise the industry and really detest how builders perceived their own contractors. On our final large commercial project, I remember having a stern conversation with the project manager of the site because he questioned one of our invoices from some variation work that we had completed. He started to question me on things like: 'how much did the cable cost?' 'How much did the other materials cost?' He went on to tell me that the labour component was too high if you were to base it off $80 per hour for a full day's work. In his eyes, it didn't match up. This was coming from an 'employee mentality' who had never operated a business before. I simply asked him: 'How did you come up with $80 per hour?' 'Who gave you those numbers?' His response was priceless: 'That's the going rate, isn't it?' I went on to give him some stern words over the phone and told him I'd explain it in further detail later that afternoon in an email, so he'd always have it on file. That way he could remember me in years to come. I never got a response from my email. Because I know he didn't have one. I also went on to tell him that $80 per hour wouldn't even cover my costs, let alone make a profit. I also told him I don't price based on an hourly rate; this is the biggest mistake people make. It's a poor business model and leaves you exposed to a plethora of potential issues where clients start to nitpick everything. You can't waste time on petty things like this.

Always base your fees on a 'set package price'. Don't expose your hourly rate and have everything itemised with a separate dollar item next to it. Have it as a holistic figure with all your inclusions under that price. The beauty of this is that if you have allowed 6 hours to complete the task, and you smash it out in 3 hours: it's a win-win for you. You have put in the work and deserve the rewards that come with it, all pending you have fulfilled your obligation to provide an exceptional service. Why is it okay for everybody else to make a profit and not you? Know your worth and stand firm with your fees, other-wise others will set it for you. You don't want to be doing work for cheap people, let alone doing stuff constantly for free. Be wise with your time and stop allowing others to dictate your worth.

Now that we have covered the importance of net profit, I'll now share with you the three most important pieces of advice that I have personally experienced and learned over the last 23 years. I wish I had this advice early on in my career. As a result, it cost me hundreds of thousands of dollars. I don't want that for you. Take it onboard and be vigilant in running your business, especially your finances.

1. **Money should never be the main focus and sole reason why you have gone into business.** You need to have a true purpose for starting a business. What drives you? Are you changing people's lives through your work? Are you providing them with a product or service that makes them feel unbelievably good? What is the core reason behind your decision? This is the fire that ignites you in the morning. It becomes your mission and because you have an underlying drive of fulfilment: everything becomes congruent. There's a strong purpose behind your actions. You understand the reasons why you're doing it: and not just hoping for the best. Once you do this, combined with providing a great service to your new or existing customers, the money will flow naturally and abundantly.

   Look, there will be times when you don't want to do certain tasks, that's inevitable. This happens in every profession. Sometimes we must do things we don't like to do, in order to reach the outcomes we desire. You need to put in the time to see exponential results. Do you think boxers love getting up at 3 am to run and train? It's not ideal, however, their eyes are on the end goal. They know what they want, and they are prepared to get in the trenches and get their hands dirty. They'll do whatever it takes because their purpose is so strong. Usually, this is to win a world title.

After you've established this, now you must dissect and know your numbers to ensure your business will be profitable. If you don't know how to do this, please hire a professional and seek advice from someone who has been there and done it for themselves. Never go in blind as you will leave yourself exposed. The game of entre-preneurship is long and challenging. You need to have the tenacity and IQ to outlast, outperform, and out-improve your competition. Never get too complacent as you can be taken out just as quickly as a sniper would take out their target. You then become another statistic. Play defensively and leave no stone unturned when it comes to your numbers. Maximise and maintain your oxygen flow: It's imperative if you want to flourish in the entrepreneurial world.

2. **If you price for profit, then I'm confident you won't be the cheapest when providing a product or service in your desired industry.** That's a good sign. Don't see this as a negative thing and don't fear big numbers. If you feel you're worth it, what's stopping you from charging it? Are you worried about what people might say? Have people told you that's impossible? Never let other people's limitations and narrow-minded thinking blind you from earning what you truly deserve. Who are they to dictate what you can or can't do in your own business or organisation? People like this are simply scared, insecure, and have a fixed mindset. They haven't seen or experienced anything like this before—that's why it's foreign to them.

    If I had a choice between two surgeons, and one of them was the best in the industry, whereas the other had just completed his training, I would pick the more experienced surgeon, even if it cost me an extra $5k. Why you ask? This is because his record and results speak volumes and his social proof is flawless. He can also deliver my desired outcome in half the time. If you want something great, be prepared to pay the price. If you can provide a solid solution, along with minimising the time it takes to fulfil the service - you have a winning formula.

When you have established your fees/rates, then you must live up to those expectations. Make it known 'why' you charge the way you do. Providing a sub-standard service and being the same as Bob down the street simply won't cut it. It won't allow you to stand apart and have a point of difference. Is it your customer service? Have you established a strong social proof with your achievements? Are you giving that extra 10% every time to ensure your clients are satisfied? Do you have a reward system in place? What do you do so that your clients remember you and don't want to go elsewhere? This doesn't need to be overcomplicated. The smallest things can make the biggest difference when it comes to customer retention. Get creative and implement something your competition isn't prepared to do. Go above and beyond; it won't go unnoticed.

3. **Whether you're an employee or business owner, you need to be frugal with your money.** Be wise and conscious of where your money is being spent. Never overcommit to expenses and unnecessary costs, especially if you're in the early stages of entrepreneurship. I'm not saying you can't give to your favourite charity or spoil yourself from time to time. However, it needs to be within your limits. Just because you've had a 20k, 50k, or 100k month doesn't mean we need to go crazy and

spend big from excitement. Be smart, strategic, and never make big financial decisions based on your emotions. Think about it first. Ask your spouse. Ask your accountant and see if the value will benefit the business or become a liability. Never make purchases just to impress and show off. You will gain nothing from this other than a lighter wallet and ongoing obligations. Become disciplined and wise where your cash is being distributed. Make it work for you, not against you.

I've realised that true wealth is much harder to obtain if you're trading your time for money. It's very hard to create great wealth in this category unless you have high-ticket coaching clients, become a popular keynote speaker, create an ongoing subscription membership with reoccurring revenue, or you have placed yourself in a niche market which enables you to charge exponentially.

When you trade time for money, you don't get paid unless you are physically there. It's the most common business model. You can create a comfortable and stable life, but it won't be generational wealth. So, the only way to combat this is to leverage other people's time and hire employees to do the work for you. This buys back your time, which you can then allocate to areas you choose to focus on, such as being creative, leading your team and being innovative. If you're in a growth phase of your business and you're struggling to keep up, yet don't have the finances to hire someone full-time, bring them on as a casual. See if it's a good fit before you fully commit. You can also look to outsource certain tasks overseas or even help you with your mundane tasks. You have to sit and think: If I gain an extra 20 hours a week by hiring someone, is it worth the money? More times than not, you'll reply yes, because you can potentially generate way more income in that time and be focusing on your strengths. Rather than performing tasks you're not strong at or provide little value. You can't wear 20 different hats and expect to have maximum velocity and output. The more weight you have on your shoulders, the less efficient you are. Therefore, your speed and growth is compromised.

Furthermore, if you have intellectual property that you create and own, this can be created once and sold over and over. All year round. Even while you sleep. This is an intelligent way of doing business. It's a very effective way of having multiple streams of income. A product-based business can also have the same effect, especially if your products are niche and are released in a high demand market. If you can capitalise on this and be the sole distributor, it amplifies the demand even more. This is something I have experienced and works very effectively. If you focus on all the chapters in this book, a plethora of opportunities and ideas will present themselves to you. Be patient and be alert. Your time will come.

9

PICK YOUR FIGHTER-JET CREW

I've been part of many teams throughout my life. I've also made the biggest mistakes, which have cost me hundreds of thousands of dollars. I've seen the highest of highs and the lowest of lows. There is one factor that has enabled me to experience the biggest victories. This factor is having a winning team in your corner—a specialised fighter-jet crew.

When you look at the best fighter pilots around the world, you'll find that they undergo years of extensive and specialised training. They are put through rigorous combat scenarios to equip them with the necessary tactical skills to become the best. They are trained to fly alone and also in packs—as a team. And when they do, it gives them safety, efficiency, and strength.

This also applies to life and business. In order to scale and reach a new level in your life or business, you have to master the level you are currently on. Sometimes we can be blinded by our own ego, beliefs, and procedures. Holistically, what worked once upon a time may not be the formula required to open the next door. Having the right crew in your corner can be the catalyst in transcending to the next destination. The power of unity is undoubtedly one of the most powerful forces. It allows you to reach serious speeds with your velocity and minimise the impact when you take a hit. Take nature as an example.

Coast redwood trees of California – one of the tallest trees on the planet, can grow to 100 meters or more in height and measures approximately 8 meters in diameter, boasting an average age of about 1,500 years. Remarkably, their roots grow only 3 to 4 meters vertically and then spread horizontally for 18 to 24 meters, intertwining with the roots of other redwoods in a grove for stability. One might expect such gigantic trees to have a deep anchoring root system, but this is not the case. Despite their shallow roots, redwoods are rarely uprooted. They endure the fiercest winds, earthquakes, fires, and storms, and can survive even prolonged flooding. The old-growth redwood forest is home to many species, creating a thriving ecosystem. How is it possible for these titans, some weighing up to 500,000 kilograms and towering over 100 meters, able to withstand resiliently for centuries?

The secret to their strength lies not in the depth but in the connection of their roots. The roots of redwood trees are intricately intertwined with those of their neighbours, creating a network of mutual support. This interconnected root system functions like a battalion of soldiers, each tree holding up and stabilising the others. They grow in close-knit groups and depend on each other not just for structural support but also for the sharing of nutrients essential for their survival. This remarkable strategy demonstrates a powerful principle - unity is strength. Much like the redwoods, having the right team around us, with members supporting one another - can enable us to stand tall and strong. By aligning ourselves with others who share our vision and challenges, we not only amplify our own stability and growth but also contribute to the resilience and advancement of the entire group.

How do we find the right individuals? It takes time and patience. Having a good level of emotional intelligence, intuition, and empathy can really benefit the outcome when selecting the correct people. Including getting the best out of your crew, continuously.

Surrounding yourself with people who are not aligned with your vision, constantly in a negative mindset, and individuals who continually gossip behind people's backs are not the tribe you want to be joining forces with. Period. These types of people will not only sabotage your pursuit for greatness, but also be a constant liability to the rest of the team or business you may be operating.

I used to hang around these types of people and found myself buying in on the negative talk. As they say, 'Talk is cheap.' If you don't have the respect to say something to that person's face - don't say it at all. For some reason, most of us have lost the art of using our mouths as a form of effective communication. We think that hiding behind a screen and talking shit about others behind their backs is tough. These individuals are just harming themselves. They have unfinished business internally, so they need to project their insecurities onto others to make themselves feel good. It's sad to see that a lot of individuals get pleasure from other people's misfortunes. I'm being very clear and blunt on this topic because you need to be street smart and have a high level of IQ when it comes to identifying the red flags.

With all love and respect, individuals who fit the above description would never make the cut in my team - I don't care how cruel that sounds. I've seen the damage it can cause, and I have found this out the hard way. Trust is earned, not given. When you're true to yourself, you know what you want. There must be no compromise when it comes to your non-negotiables, whether it be in life or business. Especially when selecting a team; your fighter-jet crew. These non-negotiables will be unique for every person reading this book. It's not a one-size-fits-all approach. Make these loud and clear from the start and set a precedent for your ongoing expectations. Never lower the bar and your standards because someone can't perform on the same level as you and the rest of the team. If you allow this to happen, you start to lose trust, respect, and credibility from the rest of the crew you are leading. Never let one individual take down an army of soldiers. Standards should consistently be rising north, not falling south.

High achievers who operate at high velocity have each other's backs. They go to battle together. They stand firm together. There's no time for negative chit-chat. They share the same vision, respect one another, and most importantly—they respect themselves. Self-respect is a true virtue. Below are the three most important attributes I look for when selecting a fighter-jet crew. You can add more, but I've found these to be pivotal in making the right choices.

1. **The first thing I look for in an individual is discipline.** I observe how they conduct themselves and their physical appearance, among other factors. Again, I'm not judging here, but you can clearly identify if someone has a daily ritual laced with discipline compared to someone who binge-watches TV, scrolls on social media all day long, is 50 kg overweight, and chooses to do nothing about it. If you are mentally and physically fit, what's the excuse? Why have you let yourself

go? When was the exact moment you gave up? You can still enjoy all the pleasures in life and remain healthy by keeping fit and exercising. It's a choice. I truly hope you find the inner strength and burning desire to start rewriting the script by hearing these truths. I want nothing more than to see you break away from the unwanted inner beliefs and cuffs holding you down. Break the cycle.

Living a life out of pity and playing the victim will get you nowhere. If you're comfortable with living a life of mediocrity, then it's probably been a waste reading this book. However, I believe that's not you. You have made the conscious choice to read through these chapters - many don't even get that far. This book is for those who want to elevate themselves and create serious velocity in their lives, not for those living in a state of comfort and laziness. When I see someone who has a daily ritual to enhance their body, mind, or spirit, it shows me they have the potential to be a good fit as a fighter-jet crew member. Consistency is a key ingredient and prerequisite to be hand-selected as part of a winning team.

2. **The second trait I look for in a person is self-respect and how they treat others.** I know multiple people who have all the money in the world, yet

they don't respect themselves, including their own team. What a toxic environment to be in daily. How do you expect your team to respect you and believe in what you stand for if you don't truly respect the most important person: YOU! Organisations like this are forever turning over staff at the same pace they change their underpants. When you let your own ego, pride, and wealth overrule your main objective, it creates an unhealthy rift, and it all starts from the top.

If the organisation's leader is a liar, cheats, and has no respect for others, it clearly shows they have big internal blocks they've never dealt with. There's been no healing. If you never heal from past traumas and limiting beliefs, you'll keep playing the devil's advocate and be a prisoner in your own destructive cycle. There will come a time when even all that money won't be able to save you. Years of internal slaughter will eventually catch up with your mind and body. It will create an imbalance, and it will give way if not attended to.

If you respect yourself enough, you'll do anything possible to get help, seek guidance, and be the first to admit and take accountability for your flaws. Once you can accept them and heal, only then can you be completely true within yourself.

Only by being truthful are you then fulfilling the 'real' you, not showcasing the fabricated version. Suppressing the truth will only work for so long. Facing it will give you true peace, which creates harmony between the mind and body. This shows true respect within yourself. It's a commendable attribute that can illuminate a phenomenal culture within a team environment. Remember, *respect is earned - not given!*

As a leader, there will be times when you receive constructive feedback from your own team. Listen carefully and take notes on everything that is discussed and brought to your attention. Take the time to reflect and think about what was said. Never respond based on temporary emotions; words can cut deep. It takes discipline and self-control to stay grounded even when things get heated.

When there's an internal issue, have the decency to sit that person down and have the conversation with him or her. Sometimes these conversations might be tough and uncomfortable. However, it shows credibility, transparency, and respect. People don't forget things like this because you make them feel wanted. A strong sense of empathy can strengthen bonds. It also could cause schisms when there's not enough.

3. **My third and final characteristic I look for in an individual to join my team is the ability to avoid unnecessary gloating.** When people start to talk themselves up and make it all about them, alarm bells go off in my head.

Look, it's completely fine to be proud of your achievements and share your biggest wins. I encourage this, but they need to be validated. The individuals who have mastered their craft and set the standard in their own industries generally don't need to gloat because their success and accolades speak for themselves.

The individuals that unnecessarily gloat, generally are the ones that call themselves:
- Self-Made Millionaires
- Head Honchos
- The Best
- Masters
- Elite
- The GOAT

The list goes on. Any successful person will tell you that they have all had help at some stage during their journey. Those who talk it up are generally the individuals who have been on the scene for five minutes and have no social proof to back their achievements and bold statements. These are the same individuals who don't have the slightest idea of accountability when they make an error. They tend to push the blame onto someone else rather than taking the hit as good leader should. They find every excuse for what could go wrong instead of finding many reasons why it could be a success. It only takes one individual to potentially cause a fracture in a team, and if left for too long, can potentially bring down an organisation.

The correct fighter-jet crew must be carefully selected. If you do, you'll considerably minimise the damage a wrong choice can cause. This even applies to contractors you hire to work on your business. You need to do your own thorough research and due diligence before engaging with their services. Never go off referrals alone. You must see their work and observe how they conduct themselves.

I remember a time when a certain accounting firm joined our team. I had previously been let down several times due to a lack of communication, negligence, and poor workmanship. After being sick and tired of all the letdowns and false promises, a friend referred me to their own firm. I thought I'd go in blind and give them a try. I figured if it worked for my friend's business, surely, they knew what they were doing and would do a great job for us too. I was completely wrong. This firm only liked to deal with big firms, so we always got brushed to the side. Our work only got done when it suited them, and we were constantly treated like peasants. Their mistakes cost us thousands of dollars. This really tested my patience. However, I took full accountability and promised myself to never go in blind again without doing my own due diligence and research.

If you have a firm or an individual conducting any type of professional service, they should be the ones constantly chasing you and giving you updates. Remember, you're paying them, not the other way around. If you find yourself being ghosted and not getting what you paid for, have a firm and direct conversation with them. If you did your job correctly at the beginning, you set the standard from the start. If you didn't, do it now and give them the benefit of the doubt with one more chance. No more. If you did set the standard and expectations from the start, then you need to break the news and part ways. No more chances. You don't deserve this. If you're paying a premium, they must deliver you a premium service. Nothing less.

Don't be disheartened if you go through many people. Trust your instincts, and the right person or team will come to you at the right time. Never be careless or rush when you must make an important decision. You don't want to be constantly paying for other people's mistakes.

Always remember: If you want to go fast, go alone. If you want to go far, pick your fighter-jet crew, and buckle up.

10

CRITICAL THINKING MATTERS

Each day, you will likely encounter several scenarios where you have to make decisions. It's part of life. Some of these decisions will be much greater than others. There will also be times when you must make critical decisions almost immediately. These decisions can make or break a person. They can also potentially be the difference between life or death.

In 2018, after completing a project in a busy local shopping centre, I decided to pay our client a visit with my wife Connie. I'd had a very hard day at work and was in two minds about whether I should go. Although I didn't feel my best, I had this huge urge and gravitational pull to go anyway. A nudge, just like the ones I explained in **Chapter 3: *INTUITION THROUGH DIVINE FORCES*.** When we arrived, I took a different path to get to our client's shop. A path I'd never walked before. I was walking this way because I wanted to get to the liquor store. My intention was to purchase a nice bottle of scotch for my client and congratulate him on their grand opening. My intentions to simply buy a bottle of scotch were drastically over-turned by witnessing a man on the ground in the middle of a busy shopping mall. He had two women by his side monitoring him.

As I walked past, none of them seemed alarmed. I simply assumed that the man had possibly fainted, and that centre management were already on their way to assist. So, I let them be without making a scene. Let's just say we should never assume.

We proceeded to walk into the shop. As I was walking to the counter to make my purchase, I heard one of the women scream. She was wailing in distress. My eyes and ears lit up like fire. I stopped everything I was doing and rushed to the man to see what was going on. After a very quick assessment, I realized the man wasn't breathing. He also had no pulse. To my amazement, one of the women had a set of chopsticks in her hand attempting to clear his airways. "Are you serious?" I asked her. I gently pushed her out of the way and told her I would take over from here. I later found out she was a doctor, which annoyed me even more. She should have known better. I automatically started CPR on the man as his life was on the line. His face started to change colour, and this was the first time I found myself in a critical situation. I had to think fast. Very fast.

The irony of this story is that I had just completed my first aid and CPR training the week before. As I had a Level 2 electrical license, this enabled me to work on the live overhead power lines you find in the street. Having a license like this made it mandatory to complete first aid training every year. It was part of our refresher course as we were constantly in a high-risk environment. The smallest pinhole in our insulated gloves had the potential to be fatal. You can't take shortcuts when working on live power.

I felt God had put me on this path at the right time to be by this man's side. As I was performing mouth-to-mouth and giving him compressions, another man by the name of Art came to assist me moments later. Art was also a volunteer from St. Johns Ambulance. We forged a great bond from the most unexpected circumstances. We were now working in unison for at least 10 minutes. By this stage, the shopping centre was crowded with patrons coming to do their late-night shopping. I remember women and kids screaming, and many of them were crying at the sight of us trying to revive this man. Not long after, as if it were from a movie scene, approximately six ambulance paramedics rushed around the corner with all their equipment, telling people to get out of the way. As they approached, I looked up at one of the leading paramedics and asked her, "Do you want to take over?" "No," she replied. "Keep going, you're doing a great job." The paramedics didn't want to break our rhythm. It also gave them time to set up the defibrillator. Once this was set up, the transition was quick. The pads were applied, and they issued several shocks to the man's body. After a few seconds, a heartbeat was felt. You could see the man's stomach rise ever so slightly. This was a great sign, but he wasn't out of the woods yet. The man was rushed to hospital and we later found out that he had open heart surgery. He had suffered a major heart attack and was extremely lucky to survive.

The paramedics and police told us if it weren't for Art and I conducting CPR so rapidly for the whole duration, there wouldn't have been enough oxygen in his body to pull through. The adrenaline I felt that day was something special. I never panicked, and I always felt I had a greater power guiding me throughout the ordeal. I started to question, had I not become an electrician and done the training, would our paths have crossed? Would I still be here saving his life? It made me question so many things. The more I went back, the more I realized that every little increment and interaction leading up to this event had its place. Its own perfect timing. One little deviation would have thrown out the whole scenario completely. However, it was meant to be. Everything happens at the right moment. At the right time. God's time.

This experience taught me the importance of critical thinking in the most unexpected situations. It's about staying calm under pressure, trusting your instincts, and using the skills and knowledge you've acquired to make quick, effective decisions. Critical thinking isn't just about solving problems in a boardroom or making strategic business decisions. It's about being prepared for the unexpected, staying composed in the face of chaos, and having the presence of mind to act decisively when it matters most.

As you navigate through life, honing your critical thinking skills will enable you to handle whatever challenges come your way. It will empower you to make decisions that can save lives, steer your business through rough waters, and ensure your personal growth and success. Remember, critical thinking is not just a tool; it's a mindset. Embrace it, and it will serve you well in all aspects of your life.

A couple of weeks later, we received a phone call from the man's wife. She invited us to visit her husband, Joe, who was still recovering in hospital. We all went to see him, and it was heartwarming to see he was doing well. Although he was extremely sore, he still managed to share a few words and a smile, which made my day.

A few months later, both Art and I received an unexpected invitation to receive an award from the NSW Governor, Her Excellency the Honourable Margaret Beazley AC KC, at a private ceremony in Sydney. The Governor handed us a plaque honouring us as 'Save a Life' Award recipients. While I didn't feel entirely comfortable receiving accolades, knowing that Joe survived was my greatest reward. However, I couldn't turn down the opportunity to meet the Governor—an amazing woman whom I respect immensely. Another part of me was proud to share this special moment with my mother, my wife, and my late father, Michael.

Critical thinking is not just a skill; it's a transformative force that can elevate your life, mindset, and business to unprecedented heights. It's the bedrock of sound decision-making, innovation, and strategic planning. In a world overflowing with information and rapid changes, the ability to think critically allows you to sift through the noise, make informed choices, and navigate complex challenges with confidence. Mastering critical thinking can be your greatest asset in both personal and professional arenas.

High pressure situations that require critical thinking can come to us in so many ways and can end up hitting you like a bullet. The question is, how will you handle it? There will be countless scenarios when you need to evaluate, assess, and analyse a situation. However, if you're not in the right headspace, your decision-making process will be jeopardized. Most times, we already know the answers within, yet we rely on external influencers to assist or sway our decisions. You need to be more aware and conscious of the information at hand. Never make assumptions based on other people's opinions. Listening to too many voices can also block the power within you. The external clutter overpowers your internal senses. Ignite the part of your brain that can create calm amidst the chaos.

Analytical thinking is a cornerstone of critical thinking. It involves evaluating data from multiple sources to arrive at the best conclusions. Analytical thinkers reject bias and strive to gather and consume information objectively. This process ensures that decisions are made based on facts and evidence rather than assumptions or prejudices. By honing your analytical thinking skills, you can tackle complex problems with clarity and precision, ensuring that your decisions are well-founded and effective.

Below, I have outlined the three most important characteristics that will equip you for a critical thinker's mindset.

1. **Be open-minded and have the ability to self-regulate in every situation.** This skill helps you analyse and process information impartially. It involves letting go of personal biases and considering all available information before reaching a conclusion. This unbiased approach allows for a more comprehensive understanding of issues and fosters a culture of inclusivity and creativity. By embracing open-mindedness, you become more adaptable and better equipped to handle diverse perspectives, which is crucial in today's

world, especially if you're leading a team. By being open-minded, it brings light to the surface with an essence of clarity. This enables you to enhance your problem-solving skills which are inherently linked to critical thinking. It emphasizes arriving at the best conclusion, in the time you have gathered all available information. Effective problem-solving requires a structured approach to identify, analyze and resolve issues. Critical thinking empowers you to tackle any problem - from workplace challenges to everyday life difficulties - with a methodical and informed approach. It enables you to break down problems into manageable parts and devise creative solutions that are both practical and attainable. Just like my experience in the shopping mall, I had to think quickly and find a solution to save a man's life. Having the ability to assess and find a solution quickly is a powerful skill that can create exponential growth and see you gain maximum velocity within your life or team environment.

2. **Having the ability to control your thoughts and set aside personal biases to reach the best conclusion.** An effective critical thinker questions the information at hand and scrutinizes favoured decisions. This self-discipline ensures that conclusions are based on rational analysis rather than emotional responses. The ancient Greek

stoics did this so well. By practicing self-regulation, you can maintain fairness and make decisions that are in the best interest of your goals and values. I suffered with this many times throughout my career, however it requires time to master. You must not jump to conclusions and essentially need to take a backward step, remove yourself from the heat and understand that decisions based on anger, rage and resentment - will not bring you a positive outcome. This does not only show little self-control, but it also gives the power back to the opposition. Having the ability to self-regulate, gives you the upper hand in your observation skills, which is another remarkable trait for critical thinkers. It helps you look beyond face value. Embrace multiple points of view and use observation to identify potential problems before they escalate. It allows for a deeper understanding of situations. Observant individuals can pick up on subtle cues and details that others might overlook, leading to more informed and comprehensive conclusions. By sharpening your observation skills mixed with your self-regulation skills, you enhance your ability to gather relevant information and make well-rounded decisions. Always be alert and conscious when observing certain people or environments. Once you observe, they'll come a time to interpret what you have witnessed. Interpretation involves evaluating and understanding data to determine its relevance and importance. Not all data is equal, and critical thinkers must discern which information is applicable to their situation. Effective interpretation allows you to draw accurate conclusions and make informed decisions based on the most relevant data. This skill ensures that your conclusions are not only logical but also applicable to your specific context. There could be many ways you might interpret certain experiences and interactions. It's important to remember that our initial interpretations may be far worse or less than first thought. Hence, why we should never make irrational decisions quickly. If you have the time to think and observe, take the time to do so.

3. **Evaluation is the ability to confidently make decisions based on the data available.** Even though critical thinking emphasizes putting biases aside, you need to be able to assess the credibility and reliability of the information you have. This involves weighing the pros and cons, considering the potential outcomes, and making a decision that aligns with your goals and values. Effective evaluation enables you to make sound decisions even in the face of uncertainty. By evaluating a situation, you then need to express it through means of constructive and effective communication. Communication is by far one of

the most important components of any facet of life. Without communication, no message will be delivered. And without the message, there is no outcome. Effective communication involves pre- senting evidence, supporting your conclusions, and explaining your reasoning clearly. This is par- ticularly important in a workplace setting where collaboration and consensus are often necessary. By honing your communication skills, you can ensure that your decisions are understood and supported by others, fostering a collaborative and productive environment. Some of the best leaders throughout history carved out a monumental path because of the way they communicated their message. Words have the ability to elevate. They can also detonate. Have the ability to convey your message with confidence and clarity. Never be shy to speak what's on your mind but do so with a critical thinker's mentality. Be strong, dominant, calm, and patient. Always hold the fort and set a solid foundation - especially when all eyes are on you. Just like my story in that shopping mall, you never know when you need to step up to the plate, take charge and think quickly.

Mastering critical thinking can profoundly impact both your personal and professional life. It equips you with the tools to navigate complex challenges, make informed decisions, and drive creativity. It sharpens your decision-making skills by enabling you to analyze situations thoroughly and consider all relevant factors. It gives you a unique lens. It also gives you the upper hand when you can master these traits and skills. This leads to more informed and effective decisions that align with your long-term goals. Whether you're making strategic business decisions or personal life choices, critical thinking ensures that you approach each decision with clarity and confidence. Not by mere fluke and chance.

In both life and business, problems are inevitable. Critical thinking equips you with the skills to tackle problems systematically and creatively. By breaking down complex issues into manageable parts and considering multiple solutions, you can resolve problems efficiently and effectively. This not only saves time and resources but also fosters a culture of continuous improvement.

In today's fast-paced world, adaptability is crucial. Having a strategic mindset enhances your ability to adapt to changing circumstances by fostering open-mindedness and flexibility. It encourages you to embrace new ideas and perspectives, making you more resilient and better prepared to navigate change. This adaptability is key to thriving in both personal and professional environments.

By intertwining all of the above intelligence, your senses are heightened. You can see things others can't see. You make the best decisions under pressure. You're no longer stuck on autopilot. The unwanted matrix program that has sucked you in for years is now gone. You're awakened to so much truth and you start to question; "Why did it take me so long to realize this?" Don't be hard on yourself when you notice a shift. The important lesson here is, making a shift (at any stage in life) is far better than not making a shift at all. Movement creates velocity, and this is the whole idea of this book. Unconsciousness creates a haze, but awareness sets your path ablaze.

By regularly examining your thoughts, beliefs, and actions, you can identify areas for improvement and strive for continual personal growth. This continuous self-improvement enhances your overall well-being and fulfillment, helping you become the best version of yourself.

To harness the power of critical thinking, you need to embrace curiosity and the art of questioning. Always ask yourself, 'What evidence supports this claim?', 'Are there alternative explanations? and 'What assumptions are being made here?'

Foster a habit of inquiry to deepen your understanding and open new avenues for discovery and innovation. Take time to reflect on your own thought processes and biases. Journaling can help you capture these reflections and track your progress. Engage in mindfulness practices to enhance self-awareness and emotional regulation.

Regularly seek feedback from trusted peers or mentors to gain insights into your thinking and behaviour.

When faced with a problem, break it down into smaller, manageable parts. Analyse each part systematically, considering all possible angles and perspectives. Just because a solution has not been found before, doesn't mean YOU can't find one. Develop different scenarios to anticipate potential outcomes and plan accordingly.

Critical thinking is a powerful tool that can transform your life and business. It enables you to make informed decisions, solve complex problems, and navigate the challenges of life with confidence and clarity. By embracing curiosity, reflecting on your thought processes, and adopting a structured approach to problem-solving, you can enhance your critical thinking skills and unlock your full potential. Remember, the journey to becoming a critical thinker is ongoing. Continuously hone your skills, challenge yourself, and never stop questioning. This commitment will set you apart, driving you towards a life of excellence and success. More importantly, it'll give you the velocity to thrive. You deserve it.

When I started to write this book, I made a list of all the topics I wanted to cover, the things I believe had the greatest impact - minus the fluff. Information that got straight to the point and that was crucial for success. You could call it, a recipe for winners. If you have gained just one gold nugget from my teachings - I will be a happy man. I want nothing more than to see you prosper and succeed. This wasn't written to give you a dose of motivation. This was written to help you elevate to your higher self.

There's no doubt I could've added many more chapters in this book, however I added the ones that I believe can have the biggest impact in your life or business. I wanted to give you more, because having maximum Velocity gives you more. I wanted this book to be different in so many ways. Not only from my experiences, but also to make you think differently. To get exponential results, you must think in an unconventional way.

More of the same will only get you more of the same. There needs to be a moment where you decide to flip the switch. I don't need to carry on and tell you that hard work and discipline is a prerequisite to achieving greatness. You already know that. Every actionable step you take, along with every defeat you encounter - takes you that one step closer. It makes you wiser and stronger and builds your courage and spirit. You need to have that relentless fire inside of you. The kind of fire that never ceases to diminish. If you mix this fire with everything else in this book - you will conquer the battlefield in your mind.

Whether you're struggling financially, suffering from mental health or stuck in a prison cell. Believe me when I tell you that you have the fire and ability to get yourself out of any situation: It all starts in the mind. Having a growth mindset will equip you with every chance needed for longevity and prosperity. It's the engine room for elevation, fulfilment, and the ability to leave a legacy.

Once you get to this level of mastery, you become something special. The version you were always meant to be. Don't fear the hurdles or consequences that may follow you on this path. Whatever happens to you is happening for you. It's all part of the script. Every moment has its place. You need to experience everything that goes into winning and having the chance of achieving maximum output in your life. Your accomplishments won't grow on their own, it needs your investment and nurturing. Never let people deviate you off your path and vision. Guard it at all costs. Regret is a heavy price, especially when you know time is not on your side.

VELOCITY

Velocity requires quickness of motion, be the cog in the wheel and start something extraordinary.

The pen is in your hand: Make it count.

Love and gratitude,
Robert Theodoridis

One of the very few photos I have when I was incarcerated. I'm here with my mum and dad. Although I may look okay, I was a very broken man during this phase of my life in 2013.

Receiving "Save-a-Life" Award from Her Excellency, Honourable Margaret Beazley, Governor of New South Wales

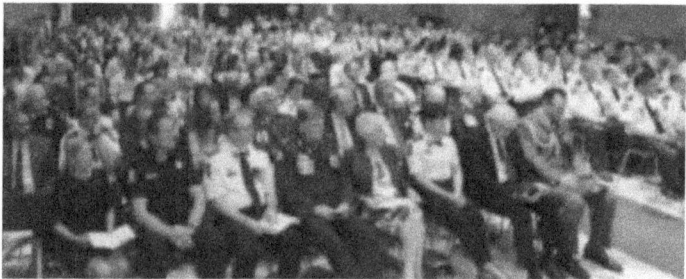

During our ceremony with the Honourable Margaret Beazley – the Governor of New South Wales: Receiving our 'Save-a-Life' Award in 2019.

With Bruce MacDonald, the then Senior Deputy Commissioner of Rural Fire Service, NSW: Along with my good friend Art Aquino after we received our awards in Sydney.

Group shot of Art, Connie and I visiting Joe and his wife while he recovered from major heart surgery. We later found out that Joe was a retired Navy Seal Diver from New Zealand, including a champion spear fisherman.

Proud moment with my wife Connie after receiving the award for the 'Best Electrical Contractor' in Australia in front of a 1000 people in Sydney.

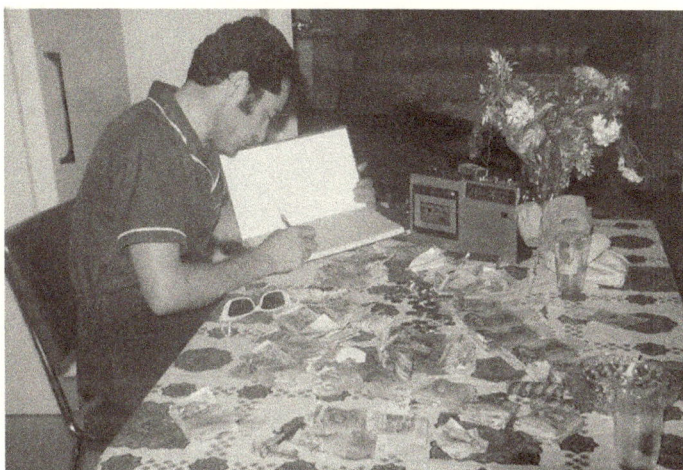

One of my favourite photos of my late father, Michael. Seen here counting the money after the shop's takings in the late 80's.

Without my parents, I wouldn't be the man I am today. I'm forever grateful for all the sacrifices they made for me.

This moment was taken after the first time I spoke on stage in front of a large audience in 2018. It was proud moment to have my father by my side.

AKNOWLEDGEMENTS

I dedicate this book to my late father, Michael. A man who taught me so much and who always showed affection. There's not a day that doesn't go by when I don't think about our deep and meaningful conversations. He was a charismatic man who had deep wisdom. I feel extremely blessed to call him my father and it was an honour to be there holding him for his final breaths. Although I've made the biggest mistakes, he always showed compassion and stood by my side like a true soldier. I will always be indebted to you and mum for your love and support. Until we meet again.

To my mum Vicki. Thank you for being such a huge part of my life. You have showed me nothing but love and support. Your selflessness and generosity over the years cannot be matched. You are a true testament of how a mother should be. I have nothing but fond memories of you throughout my whole life and I'm truly blessed to have you close to me. A mother's love cannot be broken, and I will always be there to support you. Thank you for everything you have done for me up until now - I love you.

To my beautiful wife Connie, where do I start. You're an amazing woman with an contagious personality. You always have the ability to lift me up, even in the toughest moments. Your smile, energy and wisdom are infectious. You have an exceptional mind that enables you to touch so many lives. I'm blessed to have you in my life, and I can't thank you enough for the support you have given me over the years. There is no way I would've achieved the biggest milestones without you by my side. You're the epitome of how a lioness should be – strong, nurturing, and protective. You have a unique gift of being able to elevate those around you. Your energy lights up every room and you have impacted so many individuals – including mine. Thank you for always elevating me and supporting me through life's journey. I'm proud to call you my wife: I Love you.

To my brother Emmanuel, I want to thank you for the endless advice and guidance you have shared with me over the years. You're a man that wears his heart on his sleeve and I love that about you. I admire the way you have always conducted yourself and they way you have supported your wife and raised your two beautiful boys – who are now young men. If there was three words to describe you, they would be; integrity, respect and strength. You're an amazing man and I'm truly grateful for everything you've done for me. I'm proud to call you my brother.

To my siblings, I want to thank you for supporting me throughout my life, especially through my darkest moments. You have all played special roles during my entire journey – and for that I thank you with all my heart.